One Stroke, Two Survivors

The Incredible Journey
of Berenice and Herb Kleiman

Berenice Kleiman with comments by Herb Kleiman

One Stroke, Two Survivors
The Incredible Journey of Berenice and Herb Kleiman

Cleveland Clinic Press/January 2006
All rights reserved
Copyright ©2006 Kleiman Associates Inc.

Contact:
Cleveland Clinic Press
9500 Euclid Ave., NA32
Cleveland, OH 44195
216-444-1158
chilnil@ccf.org
www.clevelandclinicpress.org

This book is not intended to replace personal medical care and supervision; there is no substitute for the experience and information that your doctor can provide. Rather, it is our hope that this book will provide additional information to help people understand the nature of stroke and stroke recovery.

Proper medical care should always be tailored to the individual patient. If you read something in this book that seems to conflict with your doctor's instructions, contact your doctor to discuss your questions. Because each individual case differs, there may be good reasons for an individual's treatment to differ from the information presented in this book. If you have any questions about any treatment in this book, consult your doctor.

ISBN: 1-59624-006-7
Library of Congress Cataloging-in-Publication Data
Kleiman, Berenice, 1937-
One Stroke, Two Survivors: The Incredible Journey of Berenice and Herb Kleiman
by Berenice Kleiman with comments by Herb Kleiman.
p. cm.
Includes bibliographical references and index.

ISBN 1-59624-006-7 (alk. paper)
1.Kleiman, Herb. 2.Cerebrovascular disease–Popular works.
3.Cerebrovascular disease–Patients–Rehabilitation–Popular works.
4.Cerebrovascular disease–Patients–Family relationships–Popular works.
I. Title.
RC388.5.K575 2006   362.196'810092–dc22

2005028797

Authors' Contact Information: http://www.onestroketwosurvivors.com
berenice@onestroketwosurvivors.com
herb@onestroketwosurvivors.com

Credits: Cover Photography by Fred Reiner and Marc Golub

DEDICATION

We dedicate this book with love and grateful appreciation to our son, Steve, who helped us survive an unbearable ordeal, and to:

Our daughters, Kathryn and Miriam, for their encouragement

Grandchildren Jonathan, Rebecca, Zachary, and Max for their smiles

Lois and Alan Elkin for their infinite support

Otis Bush, Sara Kass, and countless friends and neighbors
for their ongoing efforts

Our special team of therapists, rehabilitation psychologist,
and physicians, inpatient and outpatient, who have steadfastly
performed the impossible

And to our long-suffering dog and cat, Dizzy and Pebbles,
who were confused by it all.

CONTENTS

Stroke Recovery Timeline   vi

Foreword by Dr. Michael Felver   viii

Prologue   1

The Beginning   3

Stabilizing   19

The Rehab Hospital   27

The Twenty-Four-Hour Furlough   45

First Month at Home   56

Transitioning to Our New Life   72

Medical Complications   79

Maneuvering through the Medical Maze   93

Caregiver's Anger   100

The Outpatient Therapy Program   111

Friends and Family   123

Food-Smart Recovery   129

Toileting Nightmares   137

Travels with Herb   146

The Costs No One Talks About   153

What Happens When the Caregiver Gets Sick   163

One Stroke, Two Survivors   168

Restoring Self-Reliance   175

Conclusion   186

Postscript   190

Acknowledgments: Key Participants in Our Journey   193

Appendices

   Words to Know   195

   Useful Resources on the Internet   198

   Herbert S. Kleiman Daily Medications   200

   Herbert S. Kleiman Summary Sheet   202

   Medications as of 3/16/04   204

   Memo of 5/18/02 to Physician Team   205

   Suggested Readings   207

Stroke Recovery Timeline

July 14, 2001	Patient has stroke. Admitted to the Cleveland Clinic.
July 16, 2001	Emergency brain angioplasty. Stents inserted into carotid and left middle cerebral arteries.
July 26, 2001	Patient transfers to stroke rehabilitation and acute care center.
August 24, 2001	Twenty-four-hour home furlough.
August 28, 2001	Discharge and return home.
September 4, 2001	Home nursing care begins (ends on 10/1/01).
September 11, 2001	First EMS run to Cleveland Clinic emergency room: left arm pain.
September 14, 2001	Second EMS run to Cleveland Clinic emergency room: dehydration and exhaustion. Patient is admitted for overnight observation and extensive blood/ultrasound testing. Left arm pain continues.
September 18, 2001	Patient passes modified barium swallow study (fourth effort).
September 26, 2001	New wheelchair finally arrives.
October 2, 2001	Patient begins outpatient therapy at stroke rehabilitation center.
March 18, 2002	Cardiac angioplasty at Cleveland Clinic; insertion of two stents.
April 24, 2002	OT and PT programs conclude.
April 30, 2002	Consult with Dr. Miriam Cohen, Union Memorial Hospital in Baltimore.

Stroke Recovery Timeline (cont'd)

May 29, 2002	Therapies resume at aquatic therapy center.
September 2002	Facial pain begins.
August 7, 2003	Attack of acute glaucoma in right eye.
August 16, 2003	Herb is trapped in MRI machine during power blackout.
December 9, 2003	Evaluation and bilateral arm training at Baltimore Veterans Hospital begin.
May 17, 2004	Training for treadmill program at Baltimore Veterans Hospital.
July 3, 2004	Completion of first draft of manuscript.

FOREWORD

Stroke! One of the most fearsome diagnoses uttered by physicians. For the majority of patients so afflicted, it is an event that forever alters the ability to live a normal life. Stroke is the fourth leading cause of death in the United States and accounts for a significant portion of the health care budget. The burden of this disease will only increase as the population ages. Stroke remains singularly disabling and its long-term outcome depressing, unlike many frontiers of the diseases of aging, where breakthroughs are improving both survival and quality of life.

This is the story of Herb and Berenice Kleiman. Herb, at sixty-six, had no thoughts of retirement, until he became paralyzed from a devastating stroke. Partnered with his wife in a successful consulting business, a proud father and grandparent, engaged in the community, and, most importantly, looking forward to many more productive years, Herb's dreams were truncated on a fateful morning in 2001. Now he has survived, and his life is very different from what he had imagined it would be. Berenice's narrative chronicling their experiences with the medical system describes the rehabilitation process, adaptation to disability, and the remaking of two shattered lives. The course now is very different from three years ago. Although this is a saga filled with frustrations, Herb and Berenice's story leaves the reader inspired by the power of love and the importance of two questions: "Why?" and "Why not?"

I was the Kleimans' initial internist and remain as a friend and consultant. And, among many others, I have helped them negotiate the path to recovery. It has not been an easy road to travel, and, frankly, most of their extraordinary success is due to dogged persistence on their part rather than medical miracles. This book provides many helpful answers while raising profound questions about why recovery from a stroke cannot be made easier.

It is my hope that the medical system will take heed of patients' experiences such as the Kleimans'. The management of stroke and its aftermath can and should evolve into a comprehensive multidisciplinary specialty that economizes on office visits and simplifies the burden of the stroke victim and caregiver. Such an advance will not only improve the quality of life but will ultimately cost the system less, as stroke victims can more easily return to their own homes rather than to the long-term care environment of nursing homes.

Michael E. Felver, MD
Medical Director of Sub-Acute Services
THE CLEVELAND CLINIC FOUNDATION

PROLOGUE
It Was Looking Too Easy

On July 14, 2001, at around 9:00 a.m., my life turned upside down. My husband, Herb, survived a massive and debilitating stroke. Our world today is totally unrelated to the past. Energies that we previously focused on family, business, hobbies, and our community now converge on rehabilitation and recovery.

I have lost—temporarily or permanently—my mate, best friend, and business partner. I lost the man who walked the dog on rainy nights, cleared the dishes, and fixed what needed fixing. I miss the concerts, plays, intellectual discussions, and the long driving trips we shared. I worry about who will be my caregiver, should I ever need one. And I miss making love and the intimacy that comes from being held with two arms. This total loss is so incredible, so inconceivable that I refuse to accept it as final.

For these first three plus years,[1] I've driven my husband and myself in a continuing effort to further his recovery. As we inch our way forward, the process seems frustrating, agonizingly slow, and sometimes beyond our capabilities. But we keep going because the alternatives are worse.

Stroke survival lacks a well-defined road map. Even professionals report little patterning. No two strokes are the same; no two patients follow an exact progression. Projections are, at best, educated guesswork, but I believe that our dogged resolve and hard work will beat pessimistic percentages. Indeed Herb has already made remarkable advances.

Forty-one years ago Herb and I vowed that we would not live our lives based on numbers, clichés, or societal molds. We didn't then, and we haven't now. The poststroke journey is not easy, and we continue to encounter setbacks. Along the way, Herb remains ambivalent about his own progress.[2]

Was it worth the time and trouble to not "warehouse" me? The question has been ever present since I first came home. My moods are erratic, ranging from complete despondency to a more hopeful outlook. At the bleakest

---

[1] *Although our journey is continuing, we focus most of our story on the initial 3-1/2 years.*
[2] *Herb's comments are in dark italics.*

extreme is the concern that I'm simply a burden, not only to my wife but also to anyone lending a hand.

As wife and caregiver I, too, wrestle with questions. When do I acknowledge "enough is enough" and no longer demand continued improvement? At what point do I back off and let Herb choose an easier existence, whether that be facing his wheelchair to the wall, working at his crossword puzzle, or vegetating in front of the television set?

More determined than my husband, I continue to push exercise, experimental therapy programs, seminars, and even a nutritional regimen. Our contest of wills is often abrasive. Herb would gladly trade me and everything he owns to feast on rich desserts as often as he wishes. I, on the other hand, long for him to move his right hand and become self-directed.

A good compromise would be reaching with my right hand for a piece of scrumptious chocolate cake. Is that possible?

It is tempting to give up and walk away. Often I want to. I miss my independence and want to enjoy life. But I can't turn my back on my soul mate.

This book shares lessons and advice that, had we known them up front, would have made our journey much easier. We recount our experiences in two voices with sometimes differing viewpoints. Mine, as the caregiver spouse, are interspersed with Herb's selective comments as the stroke survivor. We hope our message reaches the family members, and especially primary caregivers, who love and care for survivors with disabling and chronic illness. Perhaps as we lift the curtain to reveal personal and family issues, our candor will ease the journey for those who follow us.

The total loss from Herb's stroke was so unacceptable, and the dour predictions so limiting, that I refused from the beginning to accept them as final. Don't allow yourself to accept similar pessimism about limitations and final outcomes either.

Together Herb and I urge you to work hard and not give up hope!

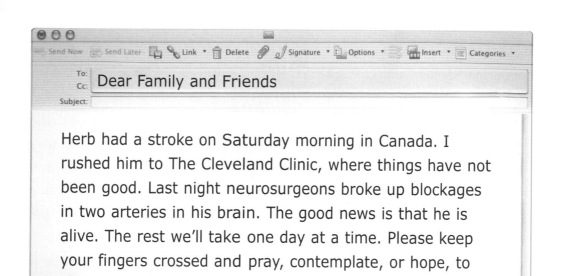

To: Dear Family and Friends
Cc:
Subject:

Herb had a stroke on Saturday morning in Canada. I rushed him to The Cleveland Clinic, where things have not been good. Last night neurosurgeons broke up blockages in two arteries in his brain. The good news is that he is alive. The rest we'll take one day at a time. Please keep your fingers crossed and pray, contemplate, or hope, to help move things along. We need your thoughts.

Berenice

CHAPTER 1
The Beginning
Strokes Happen

In retrospect, nothing seemed terribly amiss.

We had driven from our home in Cleveland up to the Shaw Festival in Niagara-on-the-Lake, in Ontario, Canada, and were staying at a favorite bed & breakfast.

This was a two-decade-long ritual for us. The town is quite small, one main street with the three theaters of the festival tucked in between tourist attractions, restaurants, and other types of stores. Its claim to fame is its location at the confluence of the Niagara River and Lake Ontario.

As theater buffs, we had been coming to the festival for many years. In a three-day weekend we often managed to pack in six and sometimes seven plays. The previous evening, at the Royal George Theatre, we had seen a play whose title will be forever lost to my memory. After chatting at the front of the theater with a couple from Cleveland, we walked to our car, and Herb drove the half mile or less to the B&B.

Yes, Herb stumbled down the front steps of the theater, but we attributed that to a degenerative neuromuscular condition that he has lived with for many years called Charcot-Marie-Tooth (CMT). We already knew that he would eventually require a cane or walker. My husband had purposely left his custom-fitted braces at home because he felt too embarrassed to wear them. Conversation walking to the car was minimal. Herb said a few things, but the evening breeze muffled his words. Rather than make an issue and ask him to repeat himself, I let it roll by. Herb has never been an immediate postperformance critic. His thoughts often take some time to coalesce, perhaps a day or more. Later in our bedroom I fell asleep reading while he watched TV.

I felt that something was a little off. My leg dragged as we walked from the theater to the car. I thought it was just a passing irregularity that would come and go. I was accustomed to living with these abnormalities. I just ignored it and didn't say anything.

Saturday morning was also not unusual. I rose early, dressed, and raced out for my favorite jog around the Major Butler burial field, a reminder of the War of 1812, when Canada and the United States did not practice a good-neighbor policy. I was back in our room not more than thirty minutes later.

The Signs

Herb was in the shower, and I remember thinking he was taking an awfully long time. My husband eagerly anticipated the B&B's breakfasts, meeting guests from around the world, discussing plays, travels, and world events over cereal, rolls, and coffee. Impatient, he often went ahead of me.

I really liked this special time. These guests were invariably visiting the Shaw Festival also, and they were usually people of diverse and interesting backgrounds with whom we could relate well.

As he was toweling off, Herb said something. I remember halting in mid-thought as I replayed his comments and thought, "Oh, my God, he's slurring his words!" As Herb repeated the phrase his words were still incomprehensible. The situation was suddenly and most awfully clear. I sat him down, told him I thought he was having a stroke, and asked him to remain still.[3] Then I ran upstairs to the dining room, where people were seated, asking—begging—everyone there for aspirin. Tucked away in the back of my mind was something I had read about taking full-strength aspirin immediately after detecting symptoms of a heart attack. I thought it might work here, too.

People at the table seemed painfully slow on the uptake. I vividly recall their puzzled expressions at the sight of this rude, sweaty American woman bursting into their conversation. Mary, the owner of the B&B, calmly directed me to a convenience store just a short drive from her home.

Jumping into the car, I pulled out, found the store, but had to wait behind a half-dozen people paying for their newspapers and leisurely passing the time with the storekeeper. The wait was interminable. I wondered how I might shake the rafters and push ahead but decided to wait my turn.

Racing back with bottle in hand, I popped two full-strength aspirin into Herb's mouth, packed up quickly, paid Mary, and threw our suitcases into the trunk before heading out the door with Herb. Although he had no other symptoms, including headache or paralysis, he followed meekly. That he didn't protest forgoing matinee tickets for that afternoon was itself worrisome and uncharacteristic. That play, too, is stricken from my memory.

Although I did not feel very sick, I decided to let Berenice take over the details of getting home. Normally, we would share the drive, she driving two hours or so, then passing the wheel to me. I was not ill or out of sorts, but I let her make all the decisions. I usually was not quite so docile, but had some inkling I'd better do as she said.

Some, including our children, have asked me how I knew so clearly that Herb was having a stroke. Perhaps it might help to explain that I had been watching, almost waiting for overt signs to emerge.

---

[3] *We had a magnet on our refrigerator from the American Heart Association listing the warning signs of stroke.*

During a rigorous trip to France three years before, both of us had become ill during the long car drive south from Paris to Avignon. I developed viral pneumonia. Herb experienced temporary facial paralysis and the beginnings of left arm pain that would haunt him for years afterward.

Medical tests and a full workup for Herb at the Cleveland Clinic immediately upon our return failed to detect any signs of stroke or problem other than viral-based Bell's palsy, which causes temporary facial paralysis. But still I worried and watched for mental and physical slowing. I remained vigilant but felt unqualified to proactively question this medical evaluation.

The Bell's palsy incident stayed with me. I thought of it as something odd that would resurface when I was cutting the lawn. Our mower was the type that required a sharp pull of the cord—very sharp. I did this with the right hand, yet the pain came to my left shoulder. It happened every time I started the mower. I conveyed this to my internist at the Clinic, but there was never a reasonable explanation.

Racing Home

Once in the car, I explained to Herb that we had two choices. We could go immediately to the nearby community hospital or take our chances and race home to the Cleveland Clinic. Ordinarily, this was a three-and-a-half-hour trip but sometimes longer with returning weekend traffic. While only a few minutes away from the small local hospital, I questioned whether they would have available the clot-busting tPA[4] injection or the skilled staff to properly administer it. I had read that there was only a three- to four-hour window for this medication to open blocked areas and to restore critical blood flow to the brain.

Having watched my mother die in a community hospital, I feared the local facility could also become a dead end. Concerns that remaining in Canada would make medical choices and subsequent commuting difficult compounded our situation.

---

[4] *TPA and other medical terms are discussed in Appendix A.*

On the other hand, if I could make it home in three hours, the full resources and medical knowledge of the Cleveland Clinic, a major tertiary care center[5] ranked as one of the top hospitals in the United States, would be available to us. In case we met a tie-up on the Peace Bridge, I was prepared to head either to Buffalo General Hospital or request a motorcycle escort at customs. Herb concurred.

We didn't make much conversation along the way, only enough to test his cognitive responses and assure me that Herb was still functioning and alert. Had there been any change or heightened urgency, I was prepared to stop. For the first time in my life, I kept hoping my lead foot would prompt whirling red lights so that we could move even faster.

I vaguely knew the location of the much closer Fort Erie Hospital along the Queen Elizabeth Way (QEW). But I kept telling myself that if I could make it over the border, Buffalo General Hospital would be larger. Fortunately, the highways on this Saturday morning were fairly empty and we decided to go all the way.

Now only a few miles from the Cleveland Clinic, Herb insisted that we stop first at home to call our internist, Dr. Michael Felver, to ask him to meet us at the emergency room. While I was on the computer pulling up phone numbers from my medical directory, Herb got out of the car, carried in luggage, opened windows, and inadvertently let the cat out.

I did not sense any imminent threat then. So I did the normal tasks upon returning home, a routine drilled into me from past trips.

Unable to reach Michael, I phoned the triage nurse, who told me to contact 911 immediately. I asked whether to give Herb more aspirin, but she cautioned me not to.

Emergency Medical Service (EMS) seemed a little dramatic after our hurried drive and might require too much of a wait. We piled back into the car. Driving turned out to be fortuitous because we learned later that the Clinic's emergency room was full and had issued a blue alert diverting all emergency vehicles to other hospitals.

---

[5] *A tertiary center offers highly specialized medical care utilizing advanced and complex procedures and treatments performed by medical specialists in state-of-the-art facilities.*

How I wish I had given Herb more aspirin. Or at least carried the bottle with us to give to him later. I never realized how much time would pass waiting for help in a medical facility.

The gravity of the situation had still not swept me up in fear. I was succumbing to my wife's overreaction, docilely following her in this adventure. Any knowledge of the negative implications hadn't occurred to me. Little did I know what lay in front of us!

The Emergency Room Wait

Herb would not let me drop him at the double doors of the emergency room and put him into a wheelchair before parking. He insisted on walking in with me. Just in front of the swinging double doors, his legs buckled and he fell to the sidewalk, scraping his knees and drawing blood.

This was typical. I have many pants ripped at the right knee attesting to this disability. It was <u>always</u> embarrassing but never before involved a serious injury.

Suddenly, police and attendants came rushing up with a wheelchair and whisked us through triage to emergency intake. I assume they based their action not on the stroke but on Herb's bleeding knees. Once ushered into a side room, our good luck ended. Medical friends had previously cautioned us not to get sick the second week in July, when new resident teams begin and staffs rotate. But a stroke doesn't choose an opportune time and now we found ourselves in the midst of this changing of the guard.

Registration took almost thirty minutes. It was already 12:30 p.m., and our four-hour window was closing when someone with a clipboard asked us when the stroke had begun. I told him nine that morning. Herb said the night before. I argued, but that was it. No anticlotting injection. I later learned that with the wrong timing tPA can cause cerebral hemorrhaging. Instead we remained in the hallway for hours before an aide took Herb for a CAT scan. Time apparently was no longer critical.

Finally placed in a small room with a blaring television set, Herb lay on a cot without further medical support or food until around 8:00 p.m., when the hospital cleared a bed and prepared to transfer him. It was disappointing to realize that the "just in time" concept prevails in medicine as well as manufacturing.

We were just beginning our first meal of the day, a McDonald's carryout that I'd fetched from an adjacent building, when word came that the bed was ready. *That sounds like we were fairly calm, doesn't it? Through the entire white-knuckle drive and up to and including the emergency room, I'd made inane conversation with Herb, trying to keep his thoughts focused. Now as I sat in the cubicle waiting endlessly, my fingernails dug into the palms of each hand, drawing blood.*

In-Hospital Care

I remained at Herb's bedside in a small semiprivate room, sitting upright in a chair all night, wrapped in a large sheet provided by a kind nurse. Early the next morning, the neurologist told us that Herb had suffered a small stroke situated in "a prime area of real estate" on the left side of his cerebrum. If conditions remained constant, he stood a good chance for recovery without much damage. That was the last positive news we heard for a very long time.

Nothing happened that Sunday morning. No nurse or resident checked in to monitor Herb. Care was custodial. Herb could walk to the bathroom, feed himself, and read the newspapers. He could also carry on a full conversation. But it became obvious to me, especially by early afternoon, that something was wrong. Increased sluggishness and decreased movement to my untrained eye indicated that his condition was deteriorating. A visiting medical friend suggested that I go to the nurses' station and firmly state that I had concerns and wished to speak with the senior resident.

It took an hour for the resident to come to our room. When I explained the situation things began to happen. Attendants immediately transferred Herb to the neurological intensive-care unit. The hospital paged an MRI[6] technician on her night off and slotted the procedure for that same evening. Again staying overnight, this time in a reclining chair with pillow and blanket, I monitored Herb's movements and breathing while awaiting the neurological report the next morning.

At 7:30 a.m. Monday, the neurologist came walking into the unit surrounded by a gaggle of half a dozen young residents. He spoke quickly to them in highly technical medical terms. I forced myself to take written notes on the back of some available hospital information papers. Apparently, the stroke was spreading. He discussed various procedures to stabilize Herb's condition, beginning with the most conservative and extending step-by-step to more invasive and riskier procedures.

The first step, he said, was to force Herb's blood pressure up to the stratosphere immediately. Increased blood flow, precipitated by medication, could possibly open blocked arteries in Herb's brain. I meekly concurred, recognizing I lacked the expertise to question his recommendation.

Within minutes nurses hooked Herb to a blinking heart monitor. He was alert, and to pass the time I read him several articles and editorials from the local newspaper. After he'd eaten an ample lunch, he raised his right arm, stretched, and said he would like to take a nap.

Lulled into a false security, I took this opportunity to quickly run home to shower, and grab some clothes and my own medications I'd not taken for the previous three days. I checked that neighbors and friends were continuing to care for our dog and cat, and then returned to the hospital. Our daughter Kathryn, whom I had called along with her siblings as soon as Herb was settled in a room, had just arrived from northern Virginia.

Herb looked as though he was still asleep. A machine monitoring his blood pressure beeped away, yet I could see that something was very wrong. He didn't respond when I tried to wake him. His eyes opened, but he was more lethargic than he'd been one hour before and had no right arm or leg movement. Apparently, nurses had not noted this change, so I called for our

---

[6] *Magnetic resonance imaging shows greater detail than a CAT scan.*

neurologist. Dr. Kerry Levin responded to the page and agreed that Herb's stroke was worsening.

More nuclear brain tests, more trips to the labyrinthine basement, so cold and intimidating that shivers ran up and down my arms and shoulders as I followed the attendant. I insisted on accompanying Herb in his roll-away cot to these tests, ostensibly because I didn't want him to wait by himself, helpless and alone, in long queues I had previously seen. Mostly, I read, held his hand, and forced limited one-way conversation. *After the guilt experienced from leaving him alone during my brief trip home, there was no way I was going to let my husband out of my sight again. It seemed abundantly clear that if I could hold his attention, he couldn't slip away and die.*

Attendants eventually moved my husband through impassable double doors for his tests and told me to wait. Only as I sat huddled by myself in a corner, the first time I was truly alone in this nightmare, did thoughts drift to the "what if my husband died..." scenario. Until now I had urged family members not to come, assuring them in my calmest voice that Herb was in excellent hands and that we had reason for hope. But time seemed to be seeping away, and the consequences were stark.

Outwardly stoic throughout the previous three days and nights as I focused on what had to be done, I could now feel my resolve crumbling. Blood pounded against my temples. I rubbed my eyes to try to hold back a throbbing headache just settling in. To keep from screaming, I clamped both hands over my mouth and stared fixedly at a small crack in the ceiling, willing back my self-discipline and control. *Why, God...why us? I desperately wanted to tear myself away from this place and this reality, and return to the way our life was before. But if that was not possible, couldn't I just dissolve into a little puff of cottonwood seed and drift someplace where there were mountains and ocean, flowers, sunshine, and calm? Far away from here.*

But there was no turning back the clock, no floating away, no escape from this impersonal dungeon of a basement filled with blaring television and frightened patients on cots and hardback chairs silently awaiting their own destinies.

Bleak reality was here, with much more to come. The devastating results of the MRI showed more clots and new blockages. Preparing us, Dr. Levin said that we might now have to consider angioplasty. He explained that the surgeon would first make an incision in the groin, then thread a device up through an artery into the neck and brain to open constricted areas. Next he would insert small wire chutes called stents, vaguely resembling little mesh tunnels, to hold open these areas indefinitely.

This invasive procedure was risky, but he hoped it would not be necessary. We had time to make that decision, he said, because Herb's elevated blood pressure might still push open these clogged areas less intrusively. He provided his cell phone number and kindly agreed to take a call from our niece, Anne Kleiman, a neurologist in New York City. Anne responded quickly, talked with Dr. Levin, and then with us. She translated medical terms, clarified the pros and cons of our remaining options, and advised us that should the situation worsen few alternatives remained other than angioplasty.

This was a new role for Annie. After her birth I had driven my niece home from the hospital. Now she was a grown woman and a knowledgeable medical professional in her own right.

And the situation did worsen—very quickly. Recognizing the gravity of Herb's condition, I placed several long-distance calls using a telephone card that by chance I carried in my wallet. I called both our son, Steve, in Los Angeles, and Herb's brother, Bill, in New York City, telling them to come immediately.

Our window was closing much faster than our neurologist or I had anticipated. *In the recesses of my mind, I kept thinking that this alert was premature. Herb was too young.... I was too young.... I didn't want to be a widow. I desperately hoped that when I awoke from this horrible dream we would both be back at the Shaw Festival just as we were before. Please, God, please God, let me wake up! Make this all a terrible mistake!*

My last call at Herb's bedside was to our younger and very pregnant daughter, Miriam, who had a ruptured relationship with her father and had not spoken with him for a number of years. I'd talked with Miriam previously and asked whether she would take a call if we came down to last minutes. I did not want Herb to die leaving her with awful regrets. She agreed. Miriam spoke briefly with Herb and, together with her husband, Jason, wished him good luck. Tears ran down Herb's eyes. Putting aside my own fears and anxieties, I hoped, if nothing else was salvaged, their exchange might help to ease Miriam's pain.

My bond with Miriam was distant to the point of no dialogue. I did not know what her feelings would be now that I was in this dire situation. Would she want to speak to me? Or would she be indifferent?

Kathryn, a new mother who traveled with her lactation pump, planned only a day trip but decided to delay her departure and take the last plane out that evening. Having her by my side was immeasurably reassuring. We exchanged few words but profound eye communication. Steadfast and outwardly calm in crisis, like her mother, she was my rock, adviser, and friend.

Although there were differences with Kathryn in earlier years, we now had a warm relationship. I felt reassured to see that she was here with me.

Another bad turn and we were suddenly face-to-face with the last of our options. Anne was back on the phone, more urgently explaining that although the stent procedure offered a long shot to limit the ultimate extent of the spreading stroke, the Cleveland Clinic was at the forefront of this new technology and it was worth the risk. Herb was conscious. I again placed the receiver by his ear. He listened to Anne and agreed.

Attendants rushed his hospital bed down the hall to the elevator. In the brief lull by the elevator, I kissed Herb for what I realized might be the last time. Then Kathryn and I ran for a second elevator.

During all the activity in this life-or-death struggle, I was somewhere between semiwakefulness and semisomnolence, drifting in and out. I did not realize the gravity of the decisions being made on my behalf.

Space-Age Technology

In the minutes it took to race to the basement operating room, I knew from rushed comments by our neurologist that Herb's chances had diminished dramatically. I thought about his living will, which restricted use of exceptional lifesaving methods, but I chose not to comply. Mutual directives were supposed to apply to our old age. This battle was immediate, and I desperately wanted my husband to live.

It was 8:00 p.m., still on Monday. Dr. John Perl, the gowned and ready neurovascular intervention specialist, explained he would perform angioplasty to appraise the situation. The carotid artery in the neck was now blocked, and he would have to open that up first.

I asked him about Herb's chances to survive. He hesitated, looked me in the eye, and said we were no longer discussing percentages. He explained there had been times after he'd performed this procedure that he could stare at himself in the mirror while shaving the next morning and feel like a hero. But there were other times he didn't want to look.

Although he had my permission, Dr. Perl said he would wake Herb up to ask his consent before proceeding. Since he did not return, I assume Herb, too, approved.

For four hours Kathryn and I sat outside the closed doors and waited. One by one, close friends joined us: Tena Rosner, who only a few months before had lost her husband, Arthur; our internist, Mike Felver; Aaron Billowitz, a psychiatrist and husband of my buddy Laurie; and Sheryl Sereda, whose teenage son, Brian, had been killed in an auto accident almost ten years before. Herb and I had shared good and bad times with each of them.

I had no idea how our friends found us in the convoluted bowels of this huge medical facility, but the group continued to grow. And we waited. We sat in a circle and held hands while we talked. I silently entreated God to return Herb to me.

Please God, help him, help him! Send him back in whatever condition and I promise to take care of the rest—just send him back!

Kathryn and friends offered enveloping love and support as we waited. Finally, around midnight, the doors opened and an exhausted Dr. Perl emerged to say that Herb had survived the placement of two stents, one in the carotid artery and another buried deep in the frontal cerebrum. But there was more: blood from a third blocked artery apparently dispersed on its own through an alternate series of blood vessels. A fourth blockage, on the opposite side, was too risky to reach under current circumstances and would be closely monitored.

Fine points and complexities failed to register. I was transfixed by the thought that despite the odds and the massiveness of his stroke, Herb was still alive. I kept muttering "Thank you, thank you, God!" as I hugged Kathryn and our friends, and sent them all home.

Seeking Help from a Higher Order

In that one brief visit home, I had turned to the Internet as a communications link to our outside world. Responses to my initial e-mail entitled "Bad News" flooded in from Japan, Israel, the UK, Ireland, France, Canada, and across the United States. Friends and family from many religious backgrounds prayed for Herb. Our nephew, Harold, in New York City stood in line to pray with a famous Hasidic rabbi. A friend in Ireland, Owen Smyth, journeyed to a rural monastery to offer his prayers for Herb's recovery. Friends from India, living in Munster, Indiana, initiated a Jain observance.

This intense knocking on God's gates must have been overwhelming. Although I had never before given much thought to the power of collective prayer, I do now. I have learned that prayer by many can defeat amazing odds. In Herb's case it did.

Herb would live. We knew that. But the extent of damage was yet to be determined. My pacts with God and Herb were only beginning to unfold.

Lessons Learned

Learn about stroke, preferably in advance.

There are two types of strokes. The first occurs when the blood supply to part of the brain is suddenly interrupted by a blood clot. The second, when a blood vessel in the brain bursts, pouring blood into the spaces surrounding brain cells. Symptoms are similar and appear suddenly. Often more than one symptom can be present at the same time.

The most important risk factors for stroke are hypertension, heart disease, diabetes, and smoking. Men statistically have a higher risk for stroke and at younger ages than women.

Recognize the first signs of stroke.

- Numbness or paralysis in the face, arm, or leg, commonly on one side of the body
- Loss of vision
- Loss or slurring of speech
- Sudden severe headache
- Balance or coordination problem
- Dizziness
- Loss of consciousness.

Seek medical help immediately.

It is imperative if you experience red-flag symptoms that you call 911 immediately. TPA, the injection that breaks up blood clots, can minimize the risk of subsequent stroke-related paralysis or death if activated within the first three hours. Beyond that limited window, the medication can have a harmful effect and precipitate massive bleeding in the brain.

Fewer than 15 percent of stroke victims recognize initial signs of their stroke and seek treatment within three hours.[7] Fewer still, below seven percent of

---

[7] *AARP The Magazine, Health Research, July/August 2004, p.13.*

stroke patients admitted to the hospital, receive clot-busting drugs.[8] Most people in circumstances similar to my husband go to bed hoping that sleep alone will improve their situation. Even if you are confused or unsure about the gravity of the symptoms, you must get to a hospital while these drugs can be effective.

Don't count on a three- to four-hour margin for action.

Don't believe, as I did, that you have a protective window of three to four hours to seek help. Medical authorities have recently revised this directive downward to two to three hours. Also, you must allow for precious time that can often be lost in the emergency room while you register and wait for help.

Carry a cell phone and prepaid telephone card.

Even if used only for emergencies, be sure you add vital medical and family phone numbers to the speed dial, keep your cell phone well charged, and carry it at all times. We wasted unnecessary time stopping at home to call our physician because I had neither his phone number nor a phone readily available. A prepaid telephone card comes in handy in health care institutions, where you must turn off the cell phone. Faster and less expensive for long distance, collect, or bill-to-a-third-number calls, it is also a good gift to ask others to bring once you are already in the hospital.

Alert family members and/or friends as soon as possible.

It is devastating to be alone during times of crisis. The support of family and friends can be comforting during long periods as you await results from medical and surgical procedures. Pragmatically, you may also need to call upon the medical expertise or advocacy of someone close to you who can translate medical terms and advise about the risks of recommended procedures.

Invite collective prayer.

Collective prayer builds strength, creates great energy, and can move mountains. I have become a believer in the power of collective prayer.

---

[8] *Ibid.*

Remain as an advocate by the side of your loved one.

Emergency rooms and hospitals, whether large or small, are busy, impersonal, even frightening institutions. No one on staff has time to pay as close attention as you can. Trust your instincts and spot problems early. Don't hesitate to call for help when necessary.

Keep a notebook.

Date and write down all medical explanations, instructions, observations, and areas of confusion or concern. The notebook provides a key and well-organized tool for subsequent reference. If you or other family members monitor the patient in shifts, your notes will be available to the next shift and allow them to add their comments.

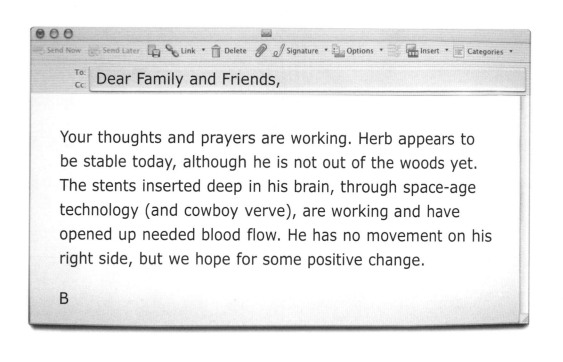

Dear Family and Friends,

Your thoughts and prayers are working. Herb appears to be stable today, although he is not out of the woods yet. The stents inserted deep in his brain, through space-age technology (and cowboy verve), are working and have opened up needed blood flow. He has no movement on his right side, but we hope for some positive change.

B

CHAPTER 2
Stabilizing

Nothing Is a Layup

At 1:00 a.m. Tuesday morning, Herb recovered in the critical care unit. The wardlike room had perhaps a dozen beds along its perimeter. Most of these were occupied. The nurses' desk was across the room and to the far right of Herb's bed.

The nurses wouldn't allow me to keep vigil by my husband's bedside as on previous nights. Instead, I was handed a blanket and advised that I might find a chair in the family lounge just down the corridor.

The Wait

As I entered this "family" room, lights were dim, and it took a little while for my eyes to adjust. A television droned. Some people were camped out on couches and chairs, and others slept on the floor, using newspapers for pillows. A single straight-back chair by the entrance was unoccupied. I slumped down there. Using my briefcase as a leg rest, I pushed backward, wrapped the blanket around me, and tried to calm down.

Even a catnap was impossible. My temples pulsated as events from the previous hours kept replaying. Thoughts were jumbled between relief and fear as my eyes fixed on the phone perched on an otherwise empty tabletop nearby. *My husband had survived complicated brain surgery. He was alive!* The nurse said that I might call in for hourly updates. On my pleading, she conceded to one brief visit during the night so I could see for myself that Herb was still breathing.

I looked around at my sleeping companions, scattered emotions mingled with curiosity as I watched a steady stream of nurses and aides feeding the vending machines. Clustered stragglers whispered quietly over cups of coffee from the twenty-four-hour McDonald's downstairs.

I wanted to doze, to allow my thoughts free rein to dream of things that were in my power to change. More than anything I wanted to will myself back to the B&B and bypass that fateful morning only four days before. But instead I remained wide awake, staring at the wall clock. *Was time my friend or foe? The next few hours could well determine whether Herb lived or died.*

The clock tracked three long hours before the nurses allowed me in to check on him. He was sleeping quietly, attached to a number of blinking monitors. His breathing was even and interspersed with an occasional snore.

By 7:00 a.m. I had permission from a critical care nurse to again keep watch by Herb's bedside.

Family Support

An hour later Herb's brother, Bill, and our sister-in-law, Thérèse, arrived from New York City. While Thérèse waited in the corridor, Bill came into the room and stood silently by Herb's head, staring down. Herb was beginning to shake off the anesthesia and showed signs of awakening.

Bill reached out, patted Herb on his chest and asked, "So, little brother, what's the capital of Nepal?" Apparently, they had played this game of geography as children.

After all that my husband had been through, my brother-in-law wanted to play a game with him? My first inclination was to kick Bill in the ankle and tell him to leave Herb alone! Instead, I stood silently and watched.

Herb partially opened one eye. He looked drowsily at his brother, and in a low voice that we could barely understand whispered, "Katmandu." At that moment both Bill and I knew that Herb's memory was still intact and that he would at least retain his cognitive function. We hugged in relief.

This was a game Bill and I played as children. He'd ask me to name any capital in the world, and I'd ask him to define any word I'd find in the dictionary.

I don't remember much about the remaining week at the clinic because even the tedious hours of waiting and the most frightening thoughts of what might happen melded together and became routinely hypnotic. Herb moved within a few days from neurological critical care back to the less intensive but still carefully monitored "step-down" unit, and finally into a room of his own. Although there was another bed in his semiprivate room, it remained unoccupied most of the time. After long uncomfortable nights on a reclining chair, with pillow and blanket provided by thoughtful nurses, I desperately wanted to climb into that extra bed and stretch out. I didn't. Too honor bound to take advantage, my poor back suffered.

I thought long and hard about that empty bed each night but superstitiously felt if I were to stretch the rules now and use something that was not mine, I might be tempting the fates. It reminded me a little of the cracks in the sidewalk that I would jump over when I was a little girl because of dire warnings.

Extent of Damage

Around seven each morning, the neurologist and his residents shuffled up the corridor room by room. Since this was the only time for updates on Herb's condition, I stood behind the door to overhear their discussion. Most of their language was unintelligible. How I longed for a medical dictionary or even access to the Internet. But I took notes and resolved to check terms later.

Herb said little. His words were slurred, raspy, and unclear. He responded to stimulus, but his cognitive function would remain in question for many weeks. Still, the "Katmandu" response held promise. Unlike the first few days in the hospital, my husband could no longer move any part of his right side, including fingers, hand, arm, leg, and foot. His head slumped as though too heavy for his neck, and saliva dripped from the corner of his slanted mouth.

Now that Herb was stabilizing, the medical and nursing staff said we had only a short window to effect positive change. Recovery would occur, if it did, only during the first three to six months. If significant progress were not made by then, we inferred that Herb would more than likely transfer to a permanent nursing home. Not a very promising forecast for my brilliant, articulate, and idea-driven husband.

Touched by an Angel

After one of these early-morning sessions with the medical team, I went downstairs to the massive clinic cafeteria to grab a cup of coffee and some breakfast. Downcast, exhausted, and despairing, I sat hunched at a corner table, not touching the tray of food. Tears trickled down my cheeks.

An attendant sweeping the floor paused at my table. I remember feeling her presence but was too immersed in sorrow to raise my head. "I'll give you a penny for your thoughts," she said.

I was so surprised to see this tiny, sparrowlike African American woman with a worn face and a warm smile leaning on her broom directly in front of me. "I'm sorry?" I hesitantly responded. I stifled the brush-off I was going to utter. Her smile was so comforting, I found myself telling her about my husband and my worries that he had extensive brain damage. She listened. "You know, if you really want your prayers answered, you'll have to show

God that you have confidence in Him. Your smile will help you to show that confidence," she said gently. I stared at her incredulously, half expecting a halo to light around her head.

We talked for a little while, and she told me her name was Rachel. Then she moved along with her work and I went back to my reflections. Later, as I rose to leave, Rachel reappeared at my side, put her arm comfortingly around my back and walked me to the elevator. I truly felt that as she did so she lifted a tremendous weight from my shoulders and gave me something that none of the physicians had to spare: hope.[9]

Buoyed with renewed expectation, I sat in the waiting room of the critical care facility and saw a handsome young man taking long strides down the corridor in my direction. Here was our son, Steve, just off the red-eye from his home in Hollywood, California. *It was so good to see him and incredibly reassuring to know that I was no longer alone during this ordeal. His hug offered the strength I needed to keep going.*

Steve would live out of his backpack for the next three months. He subsequently modified our home to accommodate Herb's needs. Even more, he provided the determination and vision that would hold me together while he and I paved the way for Herb's ensuing survival and recovery.

Steve was indispensable. Being single and the most free of our children, he had flexibility to come and go as he pleased. But this was well beyond the call of duty. In his quiet, unheroic manner, he gave Berenice a solid shoulder to lean on. In a role reversal, he was there to give his all to the two of us. Thank God for Steve!

Beginning the Long Fight Back

As Herb gained greater awareness of his surroundings, Steve was determined to challenge his father cognitively. Ever the technology whiz, he hooked up our home VCR in the hospital room and smuggled tapes and equipment back and forth in his backpack. We bought a CD player with remote control

---

[9] *I returned to the cafeteria many times looking for Rachel, both during and after Herb's hospital sojourn. I asked others about her but was told she had worked at the clinic only briefly. Almost two years later, following our daughter Miriam's suggestion, I tried to locate Rachel through the Cleveland Clinic's development office. She had slipped through the system and disappeared, leaving no phone or address.*

so Herb could play music from bed. But entertainment systems were premature. Herb needed rest and showed little interest in peripheral activities. Most of the time he preferred to doze.

Now that Herb was stabilized, the medical staff advised us to consider next steps, particularly whether we preferred to transfer him to a nursing home or rehabilitation center. Custodial care was never a consideration. Steve and I sought the best and most aggressive program in the area and queried medical friends and others in the health care community. Their response was unanimous: the MetroHealth System (Metro, for short).

Cleveland is divided in half by the Cuyahoga River. Both our home and the Cleveland Clinic are in the eastern half, and Metro is located on the west side. This division is more psychological than geographic, but Metro represented an unfamiliar area.

We declared our choice and felt fortunate that the facility had room to accept Herb as a patient. So after twelve days at the Cleveland Clinic, the time came to move Herb to Metro by ambulance. I would travel with Herb, and Steve would meet us there.

I was basically out of it during the whole time period and unaware of the many ups and downs Berenice experienced or the critical decisions she continually had to make.

Detours along the Way

Local ambulances know how to reach all local hospitals, especially the larger medical complexes. Right? Wrong! Herb was placed on a gurney in the back of the ambulance and accompanied by an attendant. I was told to sit in front with the driver. Three times over the next ninety minutes I watched her try to access a highway by going in the wrong direction. She kept repeating the same mistake. Even in his compromised condition, Herb knew his directions and could recognize what was happening. *I worried that looking out the rear window he would suffer another stroke when his natural impatience forced his blood pressure up to the ceiling.*

In my semicomatose state, I knew that something must be wrong. I could not see outside, so I depended on my other senses. The trip was taking too long, and the driver was obviously lost. These were supposed to be professionals who knew the city cold.

The driver radioed dispatch for help. Even those directions were wrong. Enough was enough. Relying on a nurse's instructions I'd received at the hospital, I told the driver how to quickly reach connecting highways. Then we followed the signs. A twenty-minute drive across town took almost two hours—without traffic.

Steve was waiting for us when we finally got up to Herb's room and eyed me as though I was responsible for getting us lost. He and Herb shared the same scowl. I remember wondering when and where we might find smooth sailing. This introduction to Metro did not portend an easy sojourn.

The nurses firmly declared that I could not stay overnight even though Herb had no roommate. With trepidation but also relief, I realized that I was about to go home to my own bed. After all this time, I wasn't sure whether my pretzel-bent back could unwind into a straight horizontal position. Herb was in a caring hospital environment dedicated to his rehab. Right?

I left Herb with a container of homemade soup a friend had brought to the Clinic, and a nurse promised to heat it up for his dinner. That didn't happen. This minor lapse foreshadowed events to come.

Returning home for my first full night in more than ten days, I turned to the washing machine and dryer for solace. For a suspended period my entire world tossed around in reckless entropy. Nothing was anchored. Nothing was in order. Washing and folding laundry presented tasks entirely within my own control from start to finish.

Over the next few days Steve and I experimented with different ways to reach Metro, seeking the shortest, most efficient route. MapQuest provided the best course. We shortened a forty-five-minute drive to thirty to thirty-five minutes, a savings that would subsequently make my life easier as I maneuvered daily and later made double round trips.

Lessons Learned

Check for limited overnight facilities for family members.

Hospitals often have small lounges tucked away for family members of patients in intensive and critical care. The nurses' station may also issue hospital blankets upon request, should you plan to remain overnight.

Seek hope in the most unexpected corners.

Physicians and nurses are trained to provide basic facts and little else. Sometimes hope can appear in the form of a smile, an act of kindness, or even a thoughtful word from a stranger.

Research your next steps.

After a patient is stabilized, rehab usually follows. Keep the process moving. In a metropolitan area you may have choices. Consider your options: do you prefer an aggressive program or one more geared toward maintenance? The hospital social worker should have information to assist in your decision, but if possible, ask the medical staff and friends for their recommendations. Accessibility is also a significant factor, should you plan to make daily visits. And, of course, cost is critical and may or may not be covered by your health care insurance.

Be sure the ambulance driver knows the way.

Assume nothing. In case your ambulance driver gets lost on the way to the rehab facility, be sure you have your own directions in hand.

Herb has transferred to an acute care rehab center for three to six weeks. Here they will help him to either regain or compensate for lost movement and speech slurring. The next few months will be critical as he works to recapture movement on his right side.

He is, as you might guess, not too happy about being restricted. But he realizes what's at stake.

Keep your thoughts and prayers coming. We need them badly. I've printed out many of your responses and read them aloud to Herb. He appreciates your messages as much as I do.

B

CHAPTER 3
The Rehab Hospital
Getting Down to Work

Brain damage from the stroke in the left hemisphere of his brain left Herb with right-sided paralysis, termed *hemiparesis* (weakness or partial paralysis). Unable to balance, walk, talk, or swallow, he could not care for himself in the most basic and personal ways, including toileting.

As I lay in my bed I thought back to thirty-five years before when I was hospitalized for several weeks following a car crash. My sense of helplessness then seemed total but in hindsight was trivial compared to this current situation. Then I survived with only a scar as remembrance.

Metro provided an intense program of therapies divided into three major categories. Physical therapists (PT) initiated a series of demanding exercises to help restore Herb's functional mobility. Occupational therapists (OT) focused on basic motor functioning, primarily involving his upper torso, along with basic tasks to ease him back into the everyday home environment. Herb's speech therapist (ST) helped him to shape thoughts, communicate ideas into words, and strengthen the face and neck muscles that facilitate swallowing.

Therapy classes met five days a week, with a rotating program on Saturday. The therapists were wonderful, dedicated professionals and generously shared their skills and enthusiasm with patients.

Therapy rooms hummed with activity. The PT area included railings, exercise beds, lifts and pulleys, and open space for walking practice. People of all ages, including a surprising number of teenagers and young adults, occupied varied electric and manual wheelchairs. Several patients moved from exercise bed to a seated position aided by a pulley. Some lay flat, performing leg lifts. Others practiced climbing stairs.

In the adjacent OT room, which reminded me of a preschool activities center, colorful equipment that resembled toys filled the shelves. An adjoining room housed a full-size kitchen and bathroom, which stood ready to help patients readapt to their home situation.

I spent many therapy sessions observing Herb, helping where I could and encouraging him and others around us as they scored new accomplishments. Some patients pushed colorful beanbags from one container into the next. One woman tried to fold laundry, slowly flattening the material with one hand and then the other. Another stroke patient hesitantly and painfully forced a beanbag up over the raised board into a box on the other side. The man made so many futile efforts that when he finally succeeded I spontaneously applauded. His face lit up with pleasure, and we made a new friend. He later wheeled himself over to our room and encouraged Herb during a low point. This gentleman, his wife, and their adult children served as role models for us.

Working Through the Regimen

Herb's first major PT accomplishment was to stand using a one-sided pyramid walker and take his first steps. It was not easy. Four attendants surrounded him. One followed behind, bringing up the wheelchair; a second held firmly onto his gait belt,[10] a strange walking aid about one and a half inches wide that buckled around him. Alligator-like teeth securely gripped the closure but easily adjusted from the opposite direction. Two other aides monitored the sides, ready to grab Herb as he fell. His face was bathed in sweat. But even he realized that this sustained walk of half a dozen steps marked a breakthrough. An intense effort, it was the first of many attempts to get him out of the wheelchair and back on his feet.

It slowly grew on me how complex are the basic and effortless things we do in life. Standing up from a bed seems like such a trivial task. The smallest of children do it, the elderly perform the act, even the simplest of souls can. So why was I having so much difficulty?

Not inclined to exercise prestroke, Herb had delighted in intellectual pursuits but spurned walking, working out, and muscle development. Over time his leg muscles atrophied and became spindly from a combination of his long-standing CMT neuromuscular condition and inactivity. Too vain to use his prescription leg braces, he had bloodied his knees in multiple falls.

Because Herb had neglected any form of exercise in the years preceding his stroke, he was unfamiliar with gym workouts, lacked a basic awareness of the way his body moved, and had little reserve strength on which to build. All three factors complicate his current efforts to walk independently.

Repetitious PT exercises are designed to build strength in leg, thigh, and hip muscles and lay the foundation for sequential advancements. With increasing strength, the patient works toward balance. Balance precedes initial efforts to walk. Walking, however slowly, eases the way toward

---

[10] *A wide belt with a special closure used by physical therapists to provide support for the patient.*

subsequent adaptation and independence. These steps, key to the patient's functioning and recovery, are equally significant from the caregiver's perspective. Achieving balance and relearning how to walk go a long way to ease the burden of transfers and lifting at home.

Although Herb had little right-leg movement, he had some—just enough—to offer hope that, with greater effort, more might develop. Michelle, his primary PT, was determined to push him further. Her efforts encouraged us.

In occupational therapy, Dawn, his therapist, placed Herb's right arm in a brace on wheels. She instructed him to use his shoulder muscle to sweep his arm across the wide table. This work, too, was tough. But in a warm, engaging, and cajoling manner she kept him focused. No activity here was demeaning. Each small movement targeted large muscle development. Herb tired easily and often worried about what would happen once rehab was over.

I despaired over what I would become once I returned home. Unable to do anything associated with my previous life, I questioned what all this work could accomplish. What would I do with my remaining years, be they a few or many?

Larissa, Herb's speech therapist, worked on word attack skills—separating sounds and attacking consonant combinations. With half his face paralyzed, his utterances were slurred, lacked volume, and sounded indecipherable. Larissa introduced exercises to help him move his tongue and facial muscles. Herb then advanced to clusters of words to improve breathing capacity and vocal power. Relearning speech became as challenging as any and all physical activity. Larissa suggested Herb approach multisyllabic words by tapping out the syllables on the handle of his wheelchair. In addition she assigned practice sheets for his off times.

Herb strained to perform the multitude of tasks and often felt discouraged by a body and brain that were slow to respond to commands or that simply did not respond at all. His therapists' professionalism and camaraderie helped sustain him during an otherwise never-never land of stroke redux.

From the beginning, I requested that a rehabilitation psychologist be added to Herb's recovery team. One day in our first week, a tall, conservatively dressed woman in tweed blazer, sensible shoes, and nametag turned to the back, appeared. With a warm, engaging smile, Dr. Elizabeth Dreben walked up to Herb and addressed him without any of the condescension I saw in the behavior of some of the nurses and attendant staff at the hospital. We chatted about her Boston background. Herb was very much a part of the discussion, asking questions and even smiling.

She was different. She was really intent on getting to know me in all dimensions. Now, three years later, she is still part of our team. There is nothing that is taboo to her, and practically nothing that she doesn't know. A real savior!

My only complaint about the therapies was that the working period was often shortened because hospital attendants arrived late to move patients back and forth to the activity centers. Unable to transport themselves to these destinations independently, patients waited in their rooms until an attendant came to wheel them. At the end of each session they waited again.

Patients in wheelchairs pending transfer clogged entrances to the therapy rooms. They resembled a parade of elephants outside the circus tent with trunks and tails linked, waiting to march in on command. After I found Herb still in his room several times after the therapy period should have begun, it was apparent that transfer inefficiency was routine.

I wanted to shout from the rooftops: doesn't anybody care? These therapy sessions were too vital to squander away fifteen-minute segments. Physicians told us repeatedly that Herb had only a limited window for recovery, and here crucial time was lost in daily transit. I resolved either to get to Metro earlier or to find someone else to move Herb. Sometimes I jogged with Herb to the therapy room to make up for lost time. It was fun to whip in and out of long corridors with the wheelchair, although nurses reprimanded me on more than a few occasions.

The Fly in the Ointment

From the very beginning, odd things about the nursing care aroused my concern. As Herb lay in his new bed, both telephone and emergency call button were positioned on his unusable right side. If something happened in the middle of the night, he had no volume or verbal ability to otherwise call for help. The floor nurse explained that the cords did not reach to the left. I crawled under the bed and made the changes myself.

Basic activities such as eating became a struggle. Failure to pass three swallowing tests[11] complicated Herb's meal choices. His liquids required starchy thickening agents, and even those caused repeated gagging and coughing. Dysphagia is a common problem among stroke survivors. It results from a partially paralyzed soft palate, weakened facial muscles, and nerves no longer able to close off the windpipe. The latter is usually an involuntary response when eating. Dysphagia can lead to infection and even suffocation when food and liquids enter the lungs.

The thickening agents exacerbated Herb's preexisting type 2 diabetes, previously controlled with oral medication. I included this information in the numerous forms I filled out and informed each physician with whom we came in contact.

Food is supposed to be easy: fill out the menu and submit weekly sheets before the designated deadline. Your selections determine the food served. That didn't happen. Herb continually received inappropriate food not on his list. Our internist and numerous dieticians had cautioned us previously to avoid juices, desserts, Ensure, and other foods heavy with concentrated starches and sugars. These now became mainstays on all his trays. The nurses explained that thickened Ensure provided vital, easily digestible nutrients.

Before each meal and at bedtime, attendants would enter the room, run a glucose test, and say, "Hmm, two hundred…three hundred…almost four hundred," for which they would then calculate and inject corresponding units of insulin. They used a sliding scale with two additional units of insulin for each fifty points of glucose above the two hundred threshold. An

---

[11] *The swallow test, which utilizes an endoscopic procedure, measures aspiration risk and suitability for oral feeding. Patients who, like Herb, have continuing dysphasia and lack the ability to swallow liquids receive a soft, smooth diet with thickened liquids.*

aide would inject as many as six units at a time when Herb's blood sugar rose above a three hundred level. I found this shocking.

I was horrified. Why was all of this necessary? Prior to his stroke and his stay at this hospital my husband had never had an insulin injection or a reading above 160. These astronomic numbers, unlike any I had seen before, indicated to me that no one was monitoring his tray or appropriately adjusting the menu to his diabetic requirements.

The institutional food was appalling with little to make it more tasteful or desirable. I couldn't recognize most of the foods I was supposed to eat, and nothing looked like it was worth the effort. I found the thickened fluids unpalatable and stopped eating and drinking.

Equally inexcusable was the hospital's failure to open packaged foods. Cereals, salad dressings, bananas, even Lorna Doone cookies came with plastic, cardboard, and natural wrappings that required two hands to open. With one-sided paralysis Herb had only one usable hand and limited mouth function to bite open the sealing. No one took time to open these for Herb, who could neither help himself nor ask for help. Aides removed the uneaten packaged foods.

I called the dietician and requested a meeting. When she came to the room about two hours after my call, she looked at the remains on the tray I'd withheld from pickup and acknowledged that mistakes had been made. Yet subsequent trays repeated the same selections. Responding to my daily calls, the exasperated dietician told me she had followed our mutually agreed-upon plan but couldn't be responsible for what assembly line workers might toss on the tray. I questioned whose responsibility it was since floor nurses and attendants claimed that it wasn't theirs.

Once again meeting with the head nurse, I insisted she hold Herb's "empty" trays for my inspection. From that day on all containers came into Herb's room unwrapped and arranged so he could feed himself. The Ensure had to remain until Herb consumed sufficient nutrients in his regular diet and passed his swallowing test.

Steve and I divided our shifts, trying to cover meals as well as most of the day and evening hours. It was impossible to sustain this demanding schedule with just the two of us.

Dealing with a depressed husband and father for long hours in a hospital room is mentally and emotionally draining. In addition to monitoring his food intake, we took turns administering in-room exercise and speech homework, often against Herb's wishes. Steve and I both tried to be upbeat and inject energy into a disheartening situation. Even at home, we could not allow ourselves to relax. "Off time" meant beginning to make the adjustments in the house for the day Herb would come home in a wheelchair, washing clothes, making phone calls, paying bills, caring for the pets, and performing a variety of other small and large tasks each evening.

We needed help but wanted more than a hired warm body to sit by Herb's bed, watch television, and offer fluids or call a nurse as required.

I e-mailed our surrogate daughter, Sara Kass,[12] who lived not far from Metro. Sara graduated from high school with our daughter Kathryn and has remained a close friend over the years. In response to my initial broadcast e-mail to inform friends and family of Herb's stroke, she responded, "Tell me when you need me." I needed Sara. She came immediately.

Sara agreed to spend two and later three afternoons with Herb. Now we could cover all three meals and in-room exercise.

Sara is someone special and has an unsinkable spirit. We love her!

But indifferent custodial care continued. Night attendants failed to respond to Herb's rings for a urinal or bedpan. He had no voice to shout, so he lay in his own waste, totally helpless, until someone bothered to enter the room. Often when I arrived in the morning I would find Herb, a formerly proud and dignified man, in tears and badly shaken.

Herb called once to tell me he'd fallen out of the wheelchair and lain on the floor for a long time. Unable to call out, he'd remained where he was until someone found him. Another time, while I was there, a nurse—not an

---

[12] *With her parents' consent we regard Sara as our chosen extra daughter.*

attendant—positioned Herb on the toilet. Since she was with him, I used this as an opportunity to find a bathroom for myself.

Returning, I found Herb sprawled on the tile floor adjacent to the toilet. I couldn't pull him up. I rang the emergency bell and ran into the hall shouting for help. The same nurse returned and sniffed petulantly when I asked her why she had left him alone for ten minutes. Once he was cleaned up and returned to his bed, I again questioned why she had left him in a precarious position knowing he had no balance. She said she would add it to my list of orders positioned on the blackboard (coincidentally just to the right of the Patient's Bill of Rights).[13]

Meetings followed with the social worker, the head nurse, and the attending physician during which I questioned the poor quality of care. Overcrowding wasn't the problem. Most patients in the stroke wing occupied single rooms, and a number of rooms were empty. It seemed to me that no one cared enough to make the situation better.

Shortly after the bathroom episode, an aide wheeled Herb off to therapy, and I sat alone in the room, crying in frustration. Another aide came in, one who was consistently kinder and gentler than the others, and patted me on the back, saying, "You know, you don't have to take this care. This is unacceptable."

I looked up in astonishment and asked her, "Whom do I go to? I've tried all the obvious people in authority." She gave me the name and phone number of her supervisor, in charge of both stroke and spinal cord floors. I dialed the extension and got the message that so-and-so was away from her desk, to please leave a message and have a nice day. I retorted that I was not having a nice day nor had I had a worry-free day since my husband entered the hospital.

Within ten minutes a dignified woman dressed in a tailored suit walked into the room, introduced herself, and sat down. I explained that, although our family was more than willing to provide assistance, the level of incompetence and indifference we'd encountered was dangerous and

---

[13] *The Patient's Bill of Rights, first adopted by the American Hospital Association in 1973 and revised October 1992, encourages institutions to list a series of patient rights and hospital responsibilities understandable to patients and their families. Positioned at the very top is the injunction "The patient has the right to considerate and respectful care."*

totally unacceptable. I laid out my litany of complaints, the same that I'd discussed previously with staffers and the physician in charge of the floor. She promised immediate changes, and the situation did improve.

Speaking later with the social worker, a sincere professional, I offered to debrief staff following Herb's discharge about our hospital experience. In our own professional lives, Herb and I were often called upon to consult for corporate executives. Rather than bad-mouth people or facilities, I intended to prepare a constructive critique. The physician and nursing supervisor declined.

Stroke rehab usually runs about four weeks. Many patients then transfer to nursing homes with rehab facilities. Steve and I wanted Herb to come home. He'd had enough hospitals. Since a supervisor was now monitoring his case and conditions had finally improved, we petitioned for an extra week or two at Metro. Herb was gaining from his therapies, and we needed more time to prepare for his homecoming.

I was in a world of my own and lost track of time in the hospital. It became a second home to me. One week seemed like another.

Connections with the Outside World

Meanwhile friends passed the word to others, who in turn responded and asked to be placed on our e-mail list. Their long, thoughtful, sometimes emotional responses reinforced my dwindling strength and energies. I kept an expanding manila folder to share with Herb during his more lucid moments and responded as often as possible, although not as frequently as recipients preferred. We decorated the hospital room with greeting cards, but the personal messages arriving in clusters by daily e-mail had even greater impact for both of us. Although I did not encourage visitors, a few slipped under the radar.

Preparing to Come Home

During the initial weeks, I begged attendants to teach us about home-care procedures, but they told me that would come later, closer to discharge. We also requested a meeting with the key members of Herb's rehab team. We felt it was time to discuss Herb's progress and their expectations.

Anxiously, Steve, Sara, and I compiled a list of questions for the August 15 meeting with the social worker and staff team in charge of Herb's case. Less than two weeks remained in the program. Admittedly, we were naive. Up until then we'd had no one with whom to discuss our concerns. But we were prescient enough to anticipate future needs.

MetroHealth Family/Team Meeting, 8/15/01

Herbert S. Kleiman's (HSK) current status

Projections for HSK recovery/rehabilitation

- Short term (six months)
- Medium term (three years)
- Long term (ten years).

Transfer from hospital back home (currently set for August 28)

- Preparations for the move home
- Structural adjustments to house
- Equipment rental/acquisition: What is the ideal package of equipment for HSK at home?
- The move home: What logistical support can the hospital provide?
- Living at home: Can a single caretaker effectively manage the patient's needs over a protracted period?
- Who performs nursing tasks such as dispensing pharmaceuticals, monitoring vital signs, and bathing?
- What frequency of physician monitoring is recommended? Would checkups always occur at MetroHealth System?
- How do we balance our independence with our use of external resources?

Continuing therapy

- What programs for physical, occupational, and speech therapies are recommended? Nutritional and psychological counseling?
- What are the advantages to outpatient therapy versus in-home visits?
- What institutions are recommended within the Cleveland area?
- What kind of program is recommended? How often are sessions, and how long would such a program last?
- What kinds of exercises can HSK perform independently at home or with caregiver?

Medicare/AARP insurance coverage for homebound care

- What criteria gauge progress? When progress ceases, does coverage end?
- Does coverage terminate if HSK leaves the house (e.g., shopping at market, visit to a park, overnight trip)?
- Home equipment provided under Medicare/AARP stipulations
- Equipment needs: electric hospital bed with sides, wheelchair, commode, shower chair, rails/ramps, glucose monitor, long-handled reaching extension, walker, equipment for travel (e.g., porta-potty)
- Other equipment covered by insurance for rental/purchase
- Other equipment not covered by insurance but a tax deduction/credit.

Miscellaneous

- Viability of overnight travel away from home
- Social work support
- MetroHealth Advantage program advantages (e.g., transport for outside therapy, parking discount)
- Caregivers' stroke support group recommendations
- Add durable power of attorney to permanent hospital file
- Obtain copy of medical records/diagnostic results
- Meet in-hospital recreation therapist? Music/art therapists?
- Request family/caregiver education (e.g., bathing, dressing of patient)
- Obtain an up-to-date list of all medications/dosages/prescription filing histories.

Steve and I knew that ramps, wheelchairs, and a chairlift for our home took time to procure. These also involved considerable expense, and I was unsure what Medicare would cover. Although we had numerous questions, we didn't get many answers. The team said they would provide us with information in due course and before discharge. Their time frame obviously did not correspond with ours. For the most part we were on our own.

Now in week five, Herb's final week, the logjam broke, and everything began to move belatedly and much too frenetically. The powers that be set the date for his "overnight furlough" abruptly for the upcoming weekend, only a few days before discharge. As a trial, Herb would come home with us for twenty-four hours, and we would assume full responsibility. We were in charge of transferring him to and from the car, movement in and around the house, medications, food, toileting, and sleeping accommodations. Without sufficient training in any of these aspects, the project seemed daunting, and we had only four days to make vital hospital-to-home arrangements.

The team of therapists had assessed our home only a few days before and raised concerns about the overall layout of the house, labeling it handicap-inaccessible. Doorways to most of the bathrooms were too narrow to accommodate the wheelchair. Our home has two stairways, with one flight leading upstairs to the bedrooms and full baths and a second downstairs to the basement office. Entrances and exits, including access to the garage, all have multiple steps. Even more worrisome, Herb had no way to exit the house by himself in an emergency.

What could we do in so little time to get our home ready for this preliminary visit? Steve and I stared at each other silently for a full minute as we calculated. Without verbally communicating, we each knew our assignments. I handed him Herb's Visa card and told him to buy whatever was necessary. We ran to our respective cars and set to work. Steve took charge of facilities and logistics. I researched reliable suppliers of home medical equipment.

Home Adaptation

Steve converted his old bedroom into wheelchair-accessible space for a hospital bed. He set off on multiple trips to Lowe's and Home Depot, returning with rolls of plastic and cable, boxes, and many other items to modify the rest of the house in preparation for his father's walking and independent wheelchair rolling. He rolled up the area rugs, removed all doors—with the exception of the downstairs bathroom door, which, I emphatically said, he could not take off—and taped heavy plastic over wall-to-wall carpeting. He moved the living room furniture into a new and closer configuration to provide wheelchair space and make room for Herb's desk with adjacent computer table. Herb would now have access to the Internet.

We agreed to jointly interview sales representatives from health care supply companies. I was glad to have Steve around to share observations because the array of characters, dress, and presentations was both disappointing and alarming. One salesman showed up with his girlfriend; another came chewing gum and casually dressed in shorts; a third grossly overestimated the cost of his chairlift (we later purchased the same lift for $4,000 less). With pressure mounting and the clock ticking, I despaired that we would not find the professionals we needed for our team.

I relegated responsibility for the last salesman to our son and returned to making calls to chairlift companies. Later, assuming the meeting had long ended, I called out to Steve, "So, have you found an honest salesman yet?"

When I came upstairs, Greg Smolik, the owner of Life Quest Medical Equipment, in Euclid, Ohio, was still talking with Steve. They shared a similar grin as they resumed their discussion about ramp choices and measured the footage from the back door through the garage.

Greg allowed Steve to borrow various ramps to see which would meet our specific needs. He also arranged for a hospital bed and other adaptive equipment, including a second wheelchair and commode[14] for the upstairs level. We decided to duplicate equipment to avoid carrying each from one

---

[14] A portable toilet that sits on the floor and has a detachable pot for dumping wastes.

floor to the next. Medicare would cover basic equipment ordered by Metro such as the left-handed wheelchair,[15] pyramid walker, and commode. But ramps, duplicate equipment, and other adaptive changes to accommodate Herb's needs were our responsibility.

In the midst of these frenzied last-minute arrangements, nurses and therapists decided it was now time to teach me how to inject heparin[16] and insulin, dress and shower Herb, and administer his exercises. They were ready with long lists of tasks and apparently unlimited time to prepare me. But this was not a good time. To meet our tight schedule, I now had to be home to accept deliveries.

Final Steps before Home Furlough

Still, I made it to the hospital three days in a row, arriving at both 8:00 a.m. and 8:00 p.m. time slots for heparin lessons. The procedure was much worse than I had anticipated. The syringe came in multiple parts and required assembly. Thoroughly confused, I had no idea why the nurse thumped her finger against the cylinder.

Only later did I learn it was to prevent air bubbles from passing through the injector into Herb's bloodstream, a potentially fatal error. *The risks involved in making a mistake were deadly. Their bundle of information was simply too much, too fast, and too late to absorb. I wasn't trained as a nurse, and none of this preparation made sense to me. My panic mode only complicated the situation.*

Herb's physical therapists focused on teaching us to transfer him from wheelchair to bed. I learned to position my left foot against his immobile right leg and use my weight to pivot him up or down to the new position. Proper transfer was vital and fraught with many dangers, including falls and back strain (my own). This transfer, which would later become a fundamental part of our routine, required many sessions until I felt sufficiently capable of initiating it on my own.

More intimidating was the transition from wheelchair to car and back. It meant shoving a wooden plank under Herb's bottom and having him slide

---

[15] *With Herb's right-side paralysis, he required a wheelchair that he could manage with his left hand. The left-side wheel contains three concentric circles that control movements forward, back, and around.*

[16] *Heparin is administered to patients along with Plavix when a rapid anticoagulant effect is required.*

across the plank and onto the car seat. If the plank were not anchored solidly he could fall; too solidly, and he could not shift onto the seat. We practiced repeatedly in a car shell located somewhere in the hospital basement.

Preoccupied and tense, I was not a stellar student. The convergence of last-minute preparations created terrible pressures. Adding to the mix, Steve took advantage of late evenings to teach me how to use Quicken, a bookkeeping software system. Herb was previously in charge of entering financial data and generating reports. Steve had just upgraded our software. In view of our many medical and home adaptation expenses, I would need accurate records for the IRS. It was essential that I master this system immediately. *There were so many things I had to do, so many new challenges demanding limitless energies and attention, so many places to be at the same time. My reserves were running on empty.*

Cornered, desperate, exhausted, I turned to the ultimate high-test fill-up: chocolate. I chomped through a pound or more of chocolate daily, ranging from big seven-ounce Hershey bars to bags of colorful M&M's and boxes of fancy chocolates—sometimes in succession. A friend sent a box of chocolate- covered potato chips and Band-Aid shaped chocolates that lasted less than an hour.

The chocolate provided both adrenaline and a feel-good sense that I would somehow survive. I didn't worry about calories. My sluggish metabolism had long since shifted into running mode and everything burned off. I was so wired that often late at night, too tired to sleep, I lay awake reading. Steve, the health guru, preferred smoking to relieve his tension. I had dropped that habit many years before and considered picking it up again. Admittedly, it was tempting and had no calories. But the chocolate did its job well and I resisted.

Then came the day of reckoning: the furlough.

Lessons Learned

Check to see that emergency call buttons are readily reachable by the patient.

Make sure that both call button and telephone are positioned on your patient's usable side of the bed and readily accessible at all times.

Participate in therapies.

Participate in formal therapies both during sessions and in subsequent room exercises. Encouragement and practice are vital to your patient's rehab success. The program also readies the caregiver for the independent home efforts that eventually follow.

Insist upon caregiver preparation by the rehab hospital.

When a disabled stroke victim returns home, family members are suddenly thrust, with little preparation, into new, stressful, and very dangerous roles as caregivers. Ask for a schedule for caregiver home preparation. If not already planned, request at least four training sessions (forty-five-minute sessions are ideal) spread through the full course of the rehab program. Avoid bundling in the final week. Also insist that your therapist team evaluate your home for wheelchair accessibility several weeks before discharge to allow needed time to arrange adaptations.

Include a rehab psychologist as part of your recovery team.

Depression, a serious medical condition that affects thoughts and feelings, is often associated with abnormal functioning of the brain. Treatment for depression can shorten the rehabilitation process, lead to a more rapid recovery, and in the long run save health care costs for both the patient and the insurance company. A rehab psychologist is trained to work with stroke patients, improve their functional ability, and ease them back into everyday life. Find one with whom both you and the stroke survivor are comfortable for the long term. The average duration of major depression in people who have suffered a stroke is just under a year.[17]

---

[17] *"Depression and Stroke," National Institute of Mental Health (NIMH); Website: http://www.nimh.nih.gov*

Identify the hospital unit head or designated person in charge.

Request that the name and phone number of this unit head be positioned in a prominent location in your patient's room. Keep a dated record of derelictions in care and treatment. Report care that is negligent or below the standards of the Patient's Bill of Rights posted in your hospital room.

Propose a team progress meeting midway through the rehab program.

Ask to meet with the full medical team, including rehab specialist, psychologist, social worker, and therapists to discuss the patient's progress and expectations. Do not allow the staff to delay this meeting until immediately before discharge. Think through and prepare a detailed list of questions.

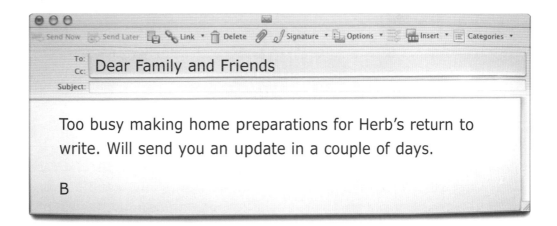

To:
Cc: **Dear Family and Friends**

Subject:

Too busy making home preparations for Herb's return to write. Will send you an update in a couple of days.

B

CHAPTER 4
The Twenty-Four-Hour Furlough

When You Think You've Reached the Lowest Level of Hell, Watch Out for the Next Descent

Herb was coming home for the first time in seven weeks. The chairlift people completed their job with difficulty. After unpacking three defective units and making repeated runs back to their warehouse, they were an hour off schedule. Their problem was a precursor to others that would haunt our weekend.

The hospital bed arrived that same morning. I'd hurriedly made it up with the latest in color-coordinated, stretchable, long twin sets from T.J. Maxx, otherwise translated as cheap and easy to wash. Not quite Martha Stewart, the room still looked comfortable. Steve set up an array of remotely controllable electronics so that his father could independently adjust lighting, television, VCR, and radio with his left hand. As a final step, I positioned a second wheelchair at the top of the stairs, adjacent to the top chairlift anchor, ready and waiting for an easy transfer. Weighing over fifty-five pounds, our primary chair was not something I intended to run up and down on demand.

Family Assistance

My brother, Alan, and sister-in-law, Lois, planned to fly in later that evening. Lois is the family medical expert. Among her best friends are top specialists at Johns Hopkins and Union Memorial Hospitals, in Baltimore. Lois figured out that we would need help during Herb's furlough. How right she was.

Steve and I picked up Herb from the hospital for his big homecoming around noon. We wedged the wooden plank between wheelchair and car and "boarded" Herb along with his pyramid walker and a big bag of medications and syringes. His nurse asked that we compile a list of problems and report back.

No one suggested that we have a twenty-four-hour nurse waiting at home. I later concluded that the purpose for this "therapeutic leave of absence," dubbed by me as "the weekend from hell," is to shock families with the overwhelming burdens of caregiving.

A nursing home was most definitely not in our plans. We intended to pull Herb away from the dehumanizing hospital environment and get him back into the world of the living as quickly as possible—hopefully, while he still had some fight left.

Thank you, God, for getting him this far. We're going to pull him back the rest of the way. Just help us do what's right and not screw this up. My thoughts jumped chaotically from excitement to anxiety and fear, then back again, along the drive home.

We entered the house through the garage, pushing the chair up our new ramps. Dizzy, our miniature schnauzer, and Pebbles, her majesty the cat, waited together in the back alcove, overjoyed to see Herb. Tears ran down his face at their welcome.[18]

Home! I shuddered at the challenge that lay in front of us now and would loom for the foreseeable future. As much as I'd wanted to come home, I wondered how Berenice and Steve would handle me. I was now fully dependent on them.

---

[18] *Stroke survivors seem very emotional, and tears flow easily.*

The thirty-five-minute trip tired Herb, and he wanted to rest. We transferred him from car to wheelchair to chairlift to upstairs wheelchair and into his waiting bed. Each transfer made me feel clumsy and inadequate. Although we said nothing explicit to each other, Steve and I wore the strain on our faces. Danger was all around us but was particularly acute at the top of the stairs, where with one misaligned move both Herb and I could tumble down.

Please, please, help me, help me. I'm afraid was my silent plea repeated endlessly throughout the day. I implored the gods of toileting not to require Herb to use the commode until I figured out how to make that difficult transfer.

Hitting the Caregiver's Wall

While Herb slept with a bicycle horn next to him to summon me when he had to use his plastic urinal, I made dinner and tried to puzzle through his lists of medications and instructions.

I tried to remain as quiet as possible. I slept much of the time without knowing of the trials hanging about me. Even the most simple efforts exhausted me. The dimensions of my vastly curtailed life still had not hit me completely.

A new meter for measuring blood sugar had arrived by mail earlier that day with another long sheet of complicated instructions. Nurses recommended that I replace Herb's trusty old OneTouch gauge because it might not be accurate for current needs. Under Medicare rules, the unit arrived "just in time" for Herb's return home but too late for hospital tutorials.

I found the directions for setting up the unit incomprehensible. A small computer-like device, it required programming with numerous inputs. And I was already jumpy. It wasn't just a matter of pricking his finger with an injector and applying a drop of blood to a swatch to produce a readout. These steps by themselves would be intimidating. But I had even greater concerns. If the glucose reading climbed above 200, I was supposed to administer insulin by correlating number of units to Herb's blood level. With a reading below 60 we had another crisis: I had to give him orange juice immediately or otherwise he might go into a diabetic stupor.

White-knuckle tension increased. I assembled the meter but couldn't program it according to the directions. It was already six o'clock on Friday evening, and lots of things had to be done quickly.

I finally placed the test strip and injector into proper position and punctured Herb's finger. The injector didn't work. Squeezing his finger repeatedly to get blood, I pinched out only a tiny bubble. Together he and I waited and watched as the device displayed an error. I did it again and again without success.

Lois and Alan arrived as backup. Lois went to work psyching out the errant meter and finally got a reading. It was a ridiculously high 256 (90–110 is generally considered within normal range). I ran down to the refrigerator and began filling the insulin syringe—another awful test because my hands were shaking so badly.

Now it was time for more medications. Then dinner. Herb was too tired to come downstairs. He ate little. I sponged him off. It was time for another glucose reading. Again the meter didn't work. Urinals…medications…were followed by the challenge of transitioning Herb from bed to commode for the first time.

Of all these new tasks, the commode was one of the most demanding. Herb, with little control of his bowels, gave me scant warning. Transferring him to the commode required that I pivot most of his weight and gently position him onto the lower, none-too-stable seat. He lacked balance and couldn't bend his knees. His right leg stood out stiffly. When he was finished, I wiped my husband for the very first time and struggled to help him stand up. Dumping the smelly pot, which fortunately came with a lid, into the toilet was another test of endurance. I realized how exposed he must feel, lacking privacy and independence for this most intimate bodily function.

This was humiliating. To have someone else performing these basic tasks for me was unthinkable, but I had no choice. I wondered if this indignity portended what my life would be like forever.

Then the time came to assemble and fill the heparin injector. The little bubbles didn't go away even after I gently tapped against the glass. With trepidation, I inserted the needle carefully into the folds of skin below Herb's stomach. If I missed and shot the heparin into the wrong place, I might kill him. I learned much later that an overdose of this powerful anticoagulant can cause massive internal bleeding and brain hemorrhage. With my heart pounding so loudly that I thought it might frighten Herb, I wondered, *Why on earth would someone like me, with so little training, be entrusted with this procedure?*

Once again the glucose monitor loomed large. I felt so sorry to repeatedly and needlessly puncture Herb's fingers. At one point I ran into the bathroom, closed the door, and sat on the floor retching into the toilet. Nausea surged up in waves. Afterward, I washed my face, counted to a hundred, and went back, resolved to try again. *He's my husband and I love him. I'll do whatever it takes! But, please, can't this all be a little easier?*

Meanwhile, Lois sought to bring order to Herb's long list of medications. She and Alan phoned pharmacies searching for plastic pillboxes to organize and store medications for two weeks in advance. Within an hour they returned with items to help me systematize our home medical activities.

Later that evening when things quieted, they told me they were taking me out for dinner. Steve, armed with war videos from Blockbuster, said he and Herb were ready to bachelor it. Apparently, Herb fell asleep almost immediately.

I directed Alan to a favorite Japanese restaurant nearby. I ordered wine, one glass after another. This was one meal I intended to partake in liquid form. Drinking with one's own brother and sister-in-law is permissible and safe, although not necessarily a mode that bespeaks command of a situation. My "dinner" eased the panic and mellowed my return. Yet silently I debated, *Must I really return home and repeat all of this again?*

Night Duty

Alone in the master bedroom that night, I slept fitfully. Much as when our children were infants and I worried about sudden infant death syndrome, I listened for every sound Herb made. Steve had set up a baby monitor by my bed with a companion unit next to Herb so that I could hear his sounds and respond quickly. He moaned and groaned repeatedly. When he wanted me he would call, "Ma, Ma." Hearing my husband call for his mother was unsettling since she had died when he was twenty-four. I wondered whether he confused us or was just unable to say my name.

Pebbles accompanied me on each successive trip. But when she saw I was going to remain, she left me on my own and went back to the comfortable warmth of our shared bed. I finished the night sitting in a rocking chair next to Herb with my feet up on the side railings.

The next day was the same. Every step, every transfer was a challenge. The fear that Herb might fall was a constant.

Lois and Alan came back that morning, bringing everything from bagels to quiche. Over coffee, they tried unsuccessfully to convince me that it was impossible for me to care for Herb by myself and that I must immediately arrange full-time care.

Herb had to get better. I was convinced he would improve only if I were the one to push him. I owed this to my husband and could not settle for less. Steve and I believed that one of the main goals in this entire recovery process was for Herb to reclaim as much physical independence as possible. His success would eventually relieve much of the physical stress on me.

Hospital Postmortem

On our return to Metro at the end of the furlough, we felt we had crossed several thresholds. Medications were now organized, an administrative function that I would rely on in the future. And we no longer needed the transfer board. Steve taught Herb to pull himself up from the wheelchair and transfer into the car by holding on to the car door frame for support while he, Steve, held the door firmly open. This procedure was easier and more secure than the board. I questioned why we were not taught this procedure by the therapists, but on further reflection understood that it involved a degree of peril they could not encourage, especially for a high-risk group in a litigious environment.[19]

Steve and I came armed with a comprehensive list of questions and concerns, distributing copies to all who asked. Well aware that only two days remained before Herb's discharge, we looked to our nurses and therapists for the answers.

The following questions stem from "friction points" encountered during Herbert Kleiman's brief visit home the weekend of August 25-26, 2001:

Patient falls to floor level

If the patient should fall down to the floor during a transfer, and assuming the patient has not sustained injury, is there a suggested procedure for lifting patient back into wheelchair?

Caregiver lifting wheelchair into trunk of car

This proved a difficult task because of the cumbersome nature and weight of the wheelchair. With outpatient therapy three times a week, the process will be repeated on an ongoing basis. Perhaps a lighter model of chair without the special axle is appropriate for out-of-house journeys? This would necessarily curtail patient's mobility during outpatient therapy.

Sitting upright

Repeated need for patient to straighten from a slouched posture to an upright position in wheelchair and chairlift seat. Request advice and exercises for patient using strong left leg to leverage body into upright position.

Patient's ability to manipulate unresponsive right leg

Repeated need for patient to position unresponsive right leg following transfers. Request advice and exercises for patient using strong left arm to lift unresponsive right leg vertically, then position foot on a footrest. Patient can currently lift right leg approximately two inches. Would a tool such as a stick

---

[19] *This car transfer procedure grew increasingly more stable with subsequent trips and helped Herb to feel that he was doing something to help himself. A very positive step in his recovery, it certainly made life much easier for me.*

with a hook on the end for grabbing shoelaces (or a wire loop tied on shoe) be a useful aid?

Caregiver "bumping up" wheelchair over a standard-height step

This proved an obstacle even with short stairs, and the situation presents itself frequently in daily life. Can you recommend a movement by which caregiver can move wheelchair up a single step without excessive back strain?

Glucose monitor, blood extraction, heparin injection review

Problems encountered testing patient's glucose levels:

1) Faulty monitor and injector

2) How can we replace both?

3) More instruction in injecting heparin and removing air bubbles.

Commode sanitary review

Request a review of strategies for proper transferring and cleaning of patient during and following commode use.

1) Transfer to commode

2) Clean patient after use (e.g., proper patient standing or semistanding positioning)

3) Change clothing as necessary from a seated position.

The first question asked by each nurse we met on our return was, "So how many times did he fall?" They seemed uniformly surprised when we said that Herb had had no falls. I wondered whether after twenty-four hours of shock probation they expected us to now place him in a nursing home.

Steve and I recognized the immensity of the challenge in front of us. The patient we were working with, my husband and Steve's father, was totally dependent. At discharge he had little, if any, mobility: he could not walk, move from the bed or chair, toilet himself or bathe, transfer, or even adjust himself in his bed on his own.

Only forty-eight hours remained to tie up all loose threads. But we had earned our battle stars and were determined to make Herb's recovery process successful. Together we drew up a list of goals to help Herb become more independent. Steve transitioned himself into the role of coach, available when we needed him but easing out gradually to return to his own life. In less than a month Herb and I would have to function without him. He drew up a list of goals for his parents:

Herbert Kleiman's Short-Term Goals

- Positioning feet into footrests on wheelchair
- Learning to test glucose and inject insulin and heparin independently [never achieved]
- Constructing a daily list of well-defined exercises to execute independently. These exercises include speech, physical therapy, and occupational therapy. Instructions will clearly indicate the task to be performed, number of sets, and number of repetitions per set.

Berenice Kleiman's Short-Term Goals

- Solving dilemma of wheelchair placement into car
- Learning to be more skillful with glucose monitor, insulin, and heparin injections
- Finding supportive help for HSK until he attains greater independence.

Advice and Consent

Lots of people encouraged me to purchase a van with a wheelchair lift. That idea seemed silly. The whole purpose of this effort was to get Herb eventually to leave the wheelchair and walk.

The same rationale guided my decision to opt for the so-called lightweight wheelchair rather than an automated one. Medicare would provide either. I considered the electric-powered chair overkill and had visions of the wheels and weight tearing up our hardwood floors. Even more to the point, my job was to force Herb to blend back into our lifestyle, and I was determined not to make this task any easier on him—or me—in the meantime.

Lessons Learned

Hire a full-time nurse to help you over the first few hurdles.

Home adjustment is challenging, whether your stroke survivor is fully or partially disabled, particularly if as caregiver you must administer complicated medications and injections. If you feel you are inadequately trained, ask others to help you. The overall situation under the best of circumstances is stressful and dangerous because of unfamiliar responsibilities, hazardous falls, and potential errors in drug administration.

Consider duplicate equipment.

Lugging a wheelchair and commode continually up a flight of stairs to a second level can easily and quickly wear out the caregiver. If you have a two-story home, arrange duplicate equipment, new or used, to ease the adjustment and strain.

Learn to operate medical devices before you go home.

Under Medicare regulations, durable medical equipment and instrumentation ordered by the hospital for the stroke survivor does not arrive until the day of discharge. This regulation leaves little time to learn new usage, programming, and applications. If your patient requires blood pressure and glucose monitoring, learn how to program and use these specific devices comfortably in the hospital before your patient comes home.

Purchase pill organizers.

Stroke survivors generally require multiple pharmaceuticals at different times of the day. Purchase a set of plastic pill organizers from your local pharmacy that sequentially divide the days of the week into segments. The organizer allows the caregiver to arrange several weeks of medication in advance while helping to avoid serious omissions and duplications.

Be patient with yourself.

The caregiver faces an abrupt change, one for which few of us are prepared. Above all, put safety first and then chart manageable expectations for yourself and your stroke survivor.

Consider a baby monitor.

Assuming the patient and caregiver sleep in separate rooms, this device relays all sounds.

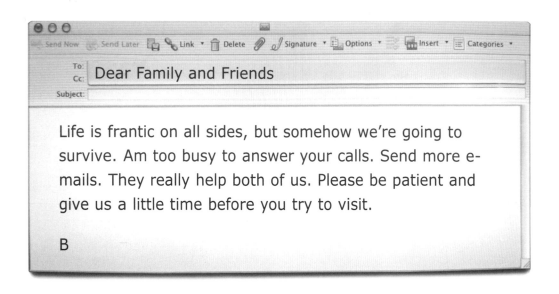

Life is frantic on all sides, but somehow we're going to survive. Am too busy to answer your calls. Send more e-mails. They really help both of us. Please be patient and give us a little time before you try to visit.

B

CHAPTER 5
First Month at Home

Sometimes Good People with the Best of Intentions Can Make a Bad Situation Even Worse

Once I had full control over Herb's diet, I eliminated starches, abandoned artificial thickeners,[20] and avoided sugars. Within the first week his glucose level dropped significantly and he no longer needed insulin. On our internist's recommendation, we discontinued heparin injections at the end of three weeks, which greatly relieved the pressure. *Pressure is a mild word. I hated the procedure!*

Wheelchair Battles

Lifting Herb's temporary wheelchair into the trunk of the car and positioning it was a huge problem. Custom-designed for left-handed control, it weighed approximately fifty-five pounds.[21] The sequenced task involved collapsing the chair (which didn't collapse easily), separating the footrests and cushion,

---

[20] *I didn't feel the risk was too great because Herb passed his swallowing test just one week later.*
[21] *Designed for one-arm use, the left wheel added considerable extra weight.*

removing the tension rod (which required me to flip the chair over and get down on my hands and knees), and then loading it from the ground into the trunk.

The chair was dead weight; I couldn't do it. Steve said that I had to because it was the only way to assure our independence. In desperation, I ran into the house and brought out a small, molded plastic table. Using that as a halfway stop, I could with great difficulty lift the folded wheelchair, rest it briefly on the table, and then thrust it into the trunk. I repeated and reversed the process a number of times, often bouncing the chair on the driveway. Steve cautioned me to bend my knees. But he refused to help me, insisting that the task was mine to master. I had several choice words for him along with my curses for the chair. *I hoped our neighbors weren't listening. I was not a happy caregiver.*

Together Steve and I wrestled with the pressure-fit tension rod that controlled the left-handed wheel. Steve compared the required movement to starting a motorcycle—something that seemed to make sense to him but did nothing for me. He taught me to twist the rod sharply forward. That worked. Later I decided not to use the difficult tension rod. The armrest was the next part to go because it was heavy and required extra trunk space. I cut other corners by storing the footrests in the trunk and using them only for outside appointments. Inside the house, Herb's feet could either dangle or rest on the floor. The daily ritual gradually became easier.

This wheelchair was still temporary. Several weeks prior to discharge, our physical therapist measured Herb as if she were fitting him for a custom-tailored suit. Since we had no preferences at that time, Metro placed the order with its normal supplier and assured me that Medicare would assume the full cost. I contacted Medicare and confirmed our coverage. I told the salesman I would not accept another one of similar poor quality. In addition to its defective braking mechanism and the difficulty of folding it, the chair kept losing screws and bolts. The supplier promised the new wheelchair would be problem free and assured me he would deliver it to our home within days following Herb's discharge.

By mid-September, about two weeks later, the new chair still had not arrived. The salesman didn't return my phone calls. A friend suggested that I contact the consumer affairs reporter for Cleveland's *Plain Dealer* newspaper and seek her help.

The reporter wrote a column about our predicament, citing the full name of the medical equipment company and listing state agencies where I might file my complaints. It was now late September.

Just after the column appeared in print, the salesman called and offered to deliver our chair the following day if I was willing to accept financial responsibility. He said he was unable to obtain Metro medical sign-offs in compliance with Medicare rules. As a second option, I could go to the hospital and obtain the sign-offs myself.

I refused both suggestions and calmly told him I would turn this matter back to the *Plain Dealer* with a detailed report of our conversation. After a pause, the salesman promised to deliver the chair the next day and work independently with the physicians to secure proper sign-offs. *I didn't feel I was bullying the guy because he had promised to get the sign-offs. That was his job, not mine. Besides Medicare regulations do not permit a recipient of home health care to leave home in the first month for other than medical appointments or a barber. How was I to race across town and run after busy physicians?*

Herb finally took command of his own wheelchair more than ten weeks after we had placed the order.

Home Care

Because of right-side paralysis, Herb was unable to raise himself in bed, turn over, sit up, dress himself, stand up, balance, walk without support, speak audibly, hold his own urinal, or control his bowel movements. He returned home deeply depressed. But he could feed himself. That was a start.

Steve was determined to rebuild his father's confidence and prove Herb could regain much more physical strength and ability than he dourly expected.

Each of us waged a separate uphill battle. Following exercise sheets provided by Metro therapists, Steve took charge of the physical and occupational skills, while I worked with Herb on speech and hand exercises. I was also responsible for urinals and commodes—not to mention medications, food, clothes, and washing.

Hemorrhaging Money

Since Herb was already sixty-six, his Medicare and AARP supplemental insurance would cover most, if not all, medical and home health care bills. I had yet to figure out sources from which to draw money to live on now that we were in sudden forced retirement. Herb and I had carefully planned our retirement program, and I was well aware of our holdings. But which investments to cash in raised complicated tax and portfolio questions requiring research and consideration. I deferred such discussions for another month until the shock of the stroke had worn off a little. Too many other issues on the front burner demanded my immediate attention.

Our business was on hold, and we needed money to pay mortgage, utilities, pharmaceuticals, and basic bills. The initial cost for home adaptation, including chairlift, duplicate medical equipment, and extensive modifications, came to over $10,000. Credit cards and checking accounts would cushion us for at least one more month, but we were suddenly hemorrhaging money with no expectation of earning more.

On top of that, I would now have to contract out many responsibilities that Herb and I had shared, including yard and handyman-type work. Herb had previously performed the large and small maintenance tasks around our home and property. Now I turned to friends and neighbors for referrals.

During Herb's hospital sojourn, neighbors arranged for lawn mowing through their service. But hedge cutting was costly. With so many other new expenses, I resolved to do that job myself once I found time.

More perplexing was an $86,000 invoice from the Cleveland Clinic for Herb's care. The mind-boggling sum was just the tip of the iceberg because

I knew bills for physicians, lab services, medical procedures, and support facilities would follow. I telephoned the hospital's financial ombudsperson and informed her that we had registered Herb's Medicare (Part A and Part B) and AARP supplemental insurance cards at his emergency admission. The statement in question disappeared but was the first of numerous other bills we continue to receive even now, usually because of data entry errors. Each requires time and effort to resolve (see Chapter 15, *The Costs No One Talks About*).

Establishing a Home Routine

Food was a priority. I was determined to build Herb's body and spirit back up and to lower his blood sugar. Slim to begin with, he had lost almost thirty pounds. He returned home emaciated, beaten down, and passive. He had little appetite and many food and drink restrictions. My challenge was to entice him into an eating pattern. I began with small amounts of his favorite heavy bean soups, reinforced with massive amounts of carrots and other vegetables. This frontline offense fortified him for Steve's physical regimen.

Twice a day, Steve made Herb lie on our wooden living room floor. With the stereo blaring Herb's favorite Broadway show tunes, Steve forced his father to lift his legs, roll from one side to the other, and then try to raise himself. After each workout Steve lifted Herb from the floor back to the wheelchair.

Steve was a terrible taskmaster. He had no mercy.

Often the two would walk with Leonard Bernstein's *On the Town* in the background. Herb grasped the pyramid walker tightly in his left hand positioning it a few inches forward. He stiffly maneuvered his right hip and leg into place, then stepped forward with the left. With this one-two-three sequence complete, he painstakingly repeated the process over and over again.

Steve insisted Herb walk, with his support, from living room through the hallway into the kitchen, dining room, and back into the living room, around fifty feet in each rotation. Together they repeated the walk again and again. Steve encouraged Herb to lift himself up from the wheelchair, but that task proved more difficult.

In his spare time Steve constructed a backyard walking aid from polyvinyl chloride (PVC) plastic pipes similar to the parallel bars used in the hospital therapy room. He hoped his father would practice walking even after he returned home to California.[22] To this day Steve tells me he had Herb on a far more rigorous exercise program than he is today and insists that I have been too soft.

In response to Herb's concern that his impaired speech showed no improvement, Steve devised a means for his father to measure his own progress. He set up a tape recorder and prepared a page from Herb's doctoral dissertation. Steve thought that if Herb continued to record his voice over a period of time, he could see the results for himself. That didn't happen, but more than a year later Herb turned on the tape recorder and listened to that first exercise. He and I were both deeply moved by the garbled tones. Like Eliza in *My Fair Lady*, we recognized the huge influence of speech therapy on his enunciation and verbal skills. Because Herb is a communicator, recognizable speech is key to regaining even a foothold in his lost world.

I was proud of my speaking ability and formerly addressed large audiences with ease. Now, with a severely constrained voice and inability to express myself, I felt imprisoned and cut off from all that distinguished me as a person.

Daily bed exercises were my responsibility and required more than an hour to complete. Herb would raise his left leg and I would lift the right. The workout alone justified my daily pound of chocolate. Herb often snoozed between sets. *The counting lulled me to sleep. Why does everything in exercise require counting?*

Prior to exercises and after medications, I sponged Herb and then carried up a breakfast tray that I placed on a crank-up table that attached to the hospital bed. While he read the *New York Times* and ate, I took Dizzy for a walk. The portable room monitor in my pocket allowed me to hear any calls for help even from down the block. In another pocket, I carried my cell phone.

---

[22] *The walking bar in our backyard remained a curiosity for neighbors, but Herb rarely used it for exercise.*

After exercises and a nap, Herb's morning was over and it was time for the next round of medications. Dressing, which was a bear, came next. The procedure was new to me and extremely difficult. Herb couldn't do much to help, and it took many weeks to develop a plan of attack. I learned to begin on the weak side and roll the shirt up to the elbow before moving to the left. Next I had to figure out that pants should go on before the braces and shoes. They simply didn't fit any other way.

Braces and shoes were another story. Formed from heavy molded plastic, Herb's braces reach from midcalf to beneath the toes. A Velcro band and buckle just below the knees serve as the single attachment. It took a balanced approach to lift the leg, guide the foot into the shell, and position both with one hand while using my other hand to fit the shoe. The braces slipped as I held the shoehorn. Herb would scowl. I fumbled and would start again. Two hands, one for the shoehorn and the other to push on the shoe, were necessary but insufficient. Both of my knees came into action as I simultaneously learned to balance his one leg and then the other. This tedious process was hard manual work. I often broke into a sweat. And, yes, I swore repeatedly under my breath.

It was hard on me as I watched her tense up. I was unable to do anything to make the task any easier. This overwhelming sense of dependency—that I couldn't take care of myself—was demoralizing for me.

Sometimes, once everything was on, Herb would wet himself. I had to remove the underwear, pants, braces, and shoes and substitute fresh pants. I bought lots of washable pants and T-shirts. Thick sweats added comfort and kept Herb as dry as possible. Although not equipped with a fly front, the elastic waistband easily stretched down under the urinal. Eliminating underwear further simplified the tedious procedure.

The urinal was a huge source of frustration. Neither of us had seen one prior to the stroke. The process requires two hands: one to hold the urinal and the other to pull down the pants and/or open the fly. With only one working hand, urine spattered and Herb required repeated changes.

Later, while Herb worked with Steve, I ran the washing machine and dryer and organized the biweekly medicine packs. Herb's many medications (fourteen in the morning, thirteen at 4:00 p.m., and four at bedtime) demanded accuracy and concentration. One mistake could create huge problems.

Running on a Constant Treadmill

Life resembled a steady treadmill those first four days home. My biggest fears surfaced when Herb used the commode. One portable unit sat in the corner of the downstairs living room and another in his upstairs bedroom. Trying to swivel and position Herb was difficult. He had no balance, and even his working leg was unsteady. I was constantly afraid he would fall. Adding to the stress, we sometimes didn't have time to move from one room to another on the same level.

Complicating this process were explosive, uncontrollable bowel movements. Several misses still stand out vividly. Herb felt so badly he sometimes cried in desperation. I tried hard not to let my revulsion show. This was my terribly sick husband. Besides, I'd raised three children and had seen it all before. Even when Steve and Sara worked with Herb, I did not stray far in case they needed me for commode duty. It was simply too intimate to involve either of them. *I saw how Herb cringed in embarrassment with me and thought how awful it would be if one or both of them had to handle this function.*

Days began around 6:30 a.m. and often ended after midnight, not counting multiple nighttime interruptions for urinal duty. I chose to wake early and carve out time to exercise and shower. Exercise included lots of stretches for my back. Late-night reading presented another release. I somehow stumbled on a five-book collection of historical fiction written by brilliant author Diana Gabaldon and found great comfort following my fictional friends through the entire series. I subsequently spoke with Ms. Gabaldon at a bookstore signing and told her how much her novels helped me survive my own ordeal.

Chocolate fueled my energy and provided a feel-good "pat on the back." It really didn't make much difference what kind of chocolate. M&M's were good; the ones with peanuts even better because they were more crunchable. The seven-ounce Hershey bars were compact and disappeared faster. For the first time in my life I could eat anything I wanted without guilt. Everything burned off. Survival took precedence over cholesterol.

Pebbles, the gentle cat, was always there to snuggle up with late at night, but sleeping solo after so many years of marriage was still a tough adjustment. Chocolate, book, and friend formed the sustenance that carried me from one day into the next. Steve found his outlet in a local gym and spent hours working out when he wasn't at home exercising his father. *But I missed my husband. The stroke aftermath was just beginning to catch up with me, and I felt a huge void.*

So did I.

Searching for Positive Signs

I desperately searched for signs of Herb's old self. I found one that made me smile and reenergized my efforts. Several days after discharge, Herb lay in his hospital bed in our son's former bedroom and said he was lonely. He patted the side of the bed and asked me to close the door and lie down. When I did, he reached out with one hand, and I could see the gleam in his eye as he fumbled with my T-shirt but persisted. Then I knew that there was much life still in my husband, but it would take enormous effort on his part, mine, and by everyone else in our working circle to bring him forward. The promising warmth and intimacy provided us both with reassurance.

Home-Nursing Interim

With four days under our belts, Herb's in-home nursing service began. Nurse Bob swept in for one hour early Tuesday morning following our arrival home. He concurred that the glucose-monitoring unit was defective. Additional home services included therapies, grooming, and social work. Different people racing in for short periods at varied times of the day tested my patience as I found myself increasingly engaged in a tug of war for authority.

Herb needed a bath at least twice a week. I was in no position to transfer him to the bath chair or move his legs over the side of the tub or, even more challenging, reverse this process on a wet floor. The home-care scheduler told me that she would have a young woman trained for this task come by about 3:00 p.m. twice a week, but her timing was ridiculous. I required help in the morning and did not want to repeat the exhausting dressing procedure multiple times in the same day. Furthermore, I wanted a man for the job and refused to yield on either point. Herb had already been stripped of his dignity, and I believed that some woman younger than our daughters would only make the situation worse.

That's when Ellie, the social worker, unexpectedly appeared the next morning. As she sat across the dining room table and patted my hand, she explained I had to learn to go with the flow. She said that the woman who would help Herb bathe was older and experienced, and as a compromise, she agreed to schedule the aide for 10:00 a.m. Ellie also advised me to relax and slow down. Health care was not a business I could organize and control. I disagreed, pointing out that my sanity and Herb's recovery were at stake. This discussion marked the first of many disagreements.

Ellie also believed that I should make time to eat breakfast as well as all other meals. She warned that I would run myself ragged and become ill, a too frequent occurrence among caregiver-spouses. *I thought she was crazy. There didn't seem to be enough time in the day between Herb's medical appointments and other needs for me to even go to the bathroom.*

The home-care occupational and physical therapists were terrific. Gayle, the OT, worked to open Herb's right hand, now a twisted fist. Patiently and with a wonderful temperament, she utilized a range of exercises. She also gifted us with our first gait belt. The hospital therapy department had used a similar belt, but I did not realize it was applicable for home use. The gait belt has facilitated Herb's walking, sitting, and transitions ever since.

Gayle also gave Herb his first home shower because the assigned person would not begin until the following week. He would otherwise have gone two weeks with only sponging. We pushed the wheelchair as far through the bathroom doorway as possible. Then Gayle and I pivoted Herb onto the shower seat and undressed him. For the shower itself, we utilized a hand control installed by Steve. Together we washed, dried, and redressed Herb. His relief was obvious.

The personal assistant who came the next week was a competent woman experienced in transitioning and showering partially paralyzed patients. Herb would now shower twice a week for the next three weeks.

Cheryl, the physical therapist, was also good. Not as insistent or as tough as Steve, who took risks and pushed Herb to his limit, she stressed walking fundamentals.[23] Steve took charge of Cheryl's homework sheets, and they reinforced one another.

The speech therapist was a bomb. He routinely canceled appointments at the last minute and imposed alternatives I could not accommodate. Halfway through the month, the agency replaced him with another therapist.

Nurse Bob gave me a calendar in which to write the therapists' different schedules. A good concept, it didn't allow enough room for the cross-outs since the therapists, nurse, and aide rarely came on schedule and often made last-minute changes. Herb's continuing complications required three or four medical appointments in the same week and precluded many of the substitutions. Ellie urged calm, but scheduling conflicts drove me up the wall. She later said the agency had never before worked with a newly discharged patient who had so many medical appointments.

Danger Lurks

Our worst accident occurred because of a last-minute substitution. The agency informed me of a bathing aide switch five minutes before the substitute arrived, leaving little opportunity for protest. She was already one hour late, and a plumber was now working in the bathroom normally used for Herb. Coincidentally, a handyman had just arrived to address a different problem. I'd initially staggered arrival times so they wouldn't conflict with Herb's shower, but now the aide and everyone else converged.

---

[23] *Here again, Steve took calculated risks to move his father forward that the therapists could not.*

The substitute, whom I assumed was experienced, said that she would have no problem taking Herb and the bench into the stall shower in the master bathroom. In the kitchen, talking with the plumber, I suddenly heard a strange, dull thud. I ran upstairs and found Herb sprawled naked on the tile floor by the shower. The aide stood above, trying to pick him up. She had a long bleeding gash down her arm. The shatterproof glass shower door was badly cracked along a vertical line, and blood was everywhere. I screamed for Steve but then remembered that he wasn't home.

Herb seemed bewildered but not in immediate pain, so I turned first to the aide. I wrapped her arm in a towel and then ran for more towels to cover Herb. The aide and I together lifted him to the wheelchair and safety. While he waited, I cleaned and bandaged the aide's arm and attempted to stop the bleeding.

Apparently, after the shower she had Herb stand up from the seat, without leg braces or shoes, and walk on the wet tile back to his wheelchair. She had no way of knowing he couldn't walk since she didn't understand his impaired speech. As he fell she threw her arm out to grab him, smashing it against the glass door.

I stared at Herb, the woman, and the bloody floor. *I wanted to shriek out that I'd had enough of these Job-like challenges. But I also recognized that the same God had answered my prayers and kept Herb alive. Instead I bit my lips and struggled to remain outwardly calm.*

I offered to call 911, but the aide said she preferred her own doctor and hurried out. Once Herb was comforted and dressed, I called the service to report the accident and left word on their answering machine. Later, because no one had called me back, I contacted our neighbor, the owner of the service, directly. Apparently, the frightened woman, worried about losing her job, had not reported the accident to her agency.

Scrubbing blood from the bathroom sink and tiles, Ellie's "go with the flow" made me angrier and angrier. *What flow? Everything associated with home care was chaotic. Herb could live on sponge baths until I found my own help.*

September 11, 2001: A Day of Infamy

September 11, 2001, came only two weeks after Herb's discharge from the hospital. That morning I, along with the rest of America, watched the horrifying destruction of the World Trade Center's towers and the growing national emergency. Steve left immediately for the Red Cross to donate blood. At midmorning, as Sara helped Herb with his bed exercises, I ran to the gas station, bank, and market. A terrorist attack could spread, and it was vital that I prepare for any future consequences.

When I returned, Sara came downstairs looking deeply troubled. After viewing television recaps, Herb complained of left arm pain much like what he'd experienced before the stroke. He was now napping quietly, but we were both worried. Even though the Cleveland Clinic had brushed off his symptoms many times before, we were well aware that shooting left arm pain could indicate a heart attack. We couldn't take any chances. I tried first to call our rehab specialist at Metro, then our internist. Neither was available. The emergency triage nurse told me to call 911 immediately. I did.

Since I'd never called EMS before, I was surprised that they came immediately with an accompanying fire truck. Here we were at noon on September 11 with sirens, lights, and neighbors standing about, faces marked with deep concern. The paramedics with their gear ran up to Herb's room. They saw nothing obvious but decided it would be best to take him to the Cleveland Clinic's emergency room. I rode in front with the driver and apologized all the way, knowing they had more to worry about on this awful day than a questionable case of muscle strain.

After numerous tests, the physician said Herb's heart was fine and he had only a urinary tract infection. He prescribed an antibiotic and sent us home five hours later. Within three days we returned to the same emergency room. Herb was now pasty faced and appeared listless. The Clinic kept him for two nights but found no obvious signs of heart problems and sent him home with a prescription for a stronger antibiotic. All the while, ubiquitous television sets showed the towers and Pentagon crumbling over and over again. Herb grew increasingly more agitated. *Bringing him home was a relief. I could finally shut off the television.*

The bombing was a horror. We knew no one involved, yet we knew everyone. I felt a deep agony.

Saying Good-bye

Steve recognized that Herb and I would have to take the next steps on our own, for better or for worse. From the beginning of September, he gently began to pull away, reappearing several times during the day to exercise Herb and tackle various problems around the house. He rewired light fixtures, replaced broken stereo speakers, interviewed handymen, and covered a range of other projects that I was oblivious to.

The end of September 2001 finally came, and it was time for Steve to return to his own life. He tested us for about a week and went to see friends in New York. He had done all he could, and we were now responsible for the remainder of our journey. Herb and I continued the difficult rebuilding process alone.

Lessons Learned

Review your health insurance coverage as soon as possible.

Your policy should include catastrophic medical coverage. Recognize the parameters of your policy(ies), particularly sections that deal with number of hospital days per incident, durable medical equipment, and therapies. Talk with a company representative to clarify any questions.

Consider a lightweight transit chair for travel.

The transit chair has less than half the poundage of a regular wheelchair, folds and lifts easily, and can remain in the car trunk. Look for a slightly used chair at substantial savings. It is ideal for appointments, assuming you prefer, as I do, not to rely on availability of wheelchairs in medical facilities. If you're unable to boost this limited weight, a van and wheelchair lift become your best option.

Purchase durable clothing.

A moderately or fully handicapped stroke survivor has basic clothing needs— primarily garments that are absorbent, easy to put on, and durable enough to withstand repeated washing. Fleece pants with stretchable waistbands are ideal and adapt easily to long periods of sitting in a wheelchair. Look for loose clothing with zippered fronts for men.

Take the hospital urinals home.

You can't have too many plastic urinals. Collect as many as you can of your survivor's urinals, which hospitals discard weekly and on discharge. You can easily disinfect and refresh them with a solution of bleach and water. If your male stroke survivor is unable to use the toilet, place urinals in convenient areas around your home. You can also purchase more urinals through a medical supply business.

Buy a backpack.

Choose one with three zippered compartments, particularly one for urinal, wipes, extra toilet paper, and plastic gloves (for the caregiver).

Schedule daily caregiver exercise time and follow it.

Repeated bending and lifting can strain your back and muscles. Even in the midst of frantic, nonstop caregiver activity, build in time and space for stretching and exercise to strengthen and relax your body. In addition, squirrel away a few personal minutes daily to use in whatever way you find relaxing and reenergizing.

Recognize the limitations of home agency care.

Medicare-provided home care offers only minimal drop-in support and little overall coverage. The biggest advantage your transition month may give you is the time to regain limited energy before beginning outpatient rehab.

Begin outpatient rehab as soon as possible.

Every day counts in revitalizing muscles and limbs. In retrospect, I believe we should have skipped home nursing and begun the outpatient program sooner.

Enlist the help of family and friends.

You can't do everything on your own, especially at the beginning. If friends aren't available, seek out a volunteer group that provides such help, perhaps through your municipality, county, church, or synagogue. You'll need help to pick up medications, prepare healthy meals, or even cover for you as you step away for a few minutes.

Place a big calendar in a prominent place.

Buy one that has the full month at a glance and daily segments large enough to list multiple activities, then keep it where you will see it often during the day. It will help you organize and limit your activities and responsibilities. One rule of thumb: if you can't fit it all into the box or in the message reminders, you may have too many activities.

Try applesauce.

When your patient has difficulty swallowing and requires many pills in multiple sizes and shapes, try mixing a few pills at a time into a teaspoon of applesauce. As Mary Poppins advises, it helps the medicine go down.

Purchase a body wash that doesn't require rinsing.

This product permits easy sponging and allows your patient to go several weeks without a full shower or bath. I wish I had known about it during the first month.

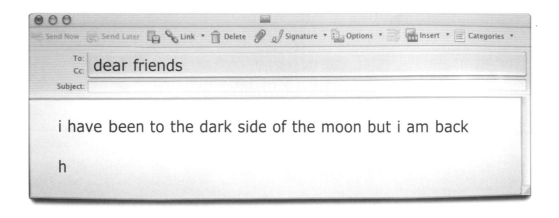

CHAPTER 6
Transitioning to Our New Life
Ties That Bind and Support—
Building a Home Team

Before leaving, Steve insisted that I hire outside support—preferably young, attractive, and dynamic individuals—to come to our home to exercise Herb several times daily. "Don't slacken the routine, and don't worry about the cost," he repeatedly said. "Spend the money." If Herb had only a limited window to improve, Steve wanted us to make as great an effort as possible.

He was also concerned about the physical and emotional toll on me from stress, disruption, and continuing caregiver demands. I needed time away to help regain my balance. "Use that time," he urged, "to give some thought to yourself and your future." Caught up in the urgency of Herb's situation, I tucked away Steve's advice and, with all my power and strength of purpose, pushed my husband forward, taking intermittent breaks but never for long periods.

Getting back to "normal" was no longer a consideration. Could Berenice ever really become adjusted to such an abbreviated life? How would she accept both me and my curtailed existence?

It was obvious I could not be both coach and wife. The caregiver role left little time or energy to be a cheerleader. Although Herb claimed he would give anything to walk unassisted and hoped to eventually mow the lawn again, he found every excuse to delay and avoid repetitive exercises. I had to find younger, more enthusiastic, and more energetic people to pick up the slack and motivate him to go forward.

Finding Support and Assistance

Sara Kass was the first member of Home Team Recovery. At the beginning, she came three mornings, from 10:00 a.m. to 1:00 p.m., but later cut back a day as she needed more time for her own business of turning young fencers into future Olympians.

She took responsibility for the slow-paced bed exercises, and sometimes during these sessions I would run to the garage and just sit in the car. No radio, phone, or interruptions. Later, with more confidence, I felt free to start the washing machine, walk the dog, or even run out for a few quick errands. Sara wasn't afraid of the urinal, so she and Herb carved out a trusting relationship.

Still, Sara wasn't enough. I desperately needed someone to bathe and groom Herb. I was fearful of transferring him from wheelchair to bath bench. Herb required support from someone well qualified in wheelchair transfers and, in the best of all possible worlds, a male. I hoped I might find a person to whom my husband could relate.

I contacted numerous home agencies and interviewed a variety of applicants, mainly women. Some were too petite, others too young. After our earlier disastrous experience, I asked the same question at the front door before inviting applicants into the house: were they experienced in transfers and bathing a partially paralyzed patient? None was. None was invited in.

Our Mr. Bush

A friend referred us to a gentleman named Mr. Bush, who had cared for her late husband. Otis Bush, then in his early seventies, was in his third postretirement stint as a surgical nurse-technician, working three days a week at University Hospitals of Cleveland. He agreed to work for us on Wednesdays and Saturdays, his off days, from 9:00 a.m. to 1:00 p.m. He and Herb quickly became best buddies.

Often when Otis arrived and carried breakfast up to Herb, I hurriedly and gratefully slipped out of the house, free to wander, shop, drive, run errands or do anything I chose in precious three- to four-hour slots. Still too tired and stressed to be with friends, I used my time away mainly to depressurize. Driving was best. I listened to the radio and often made cell phone calls to relatives and friends I had no time to speak with otherwise. But mainly I enjoyed the silence.

I made every effort to follow Steve's recommendation that we hire two or three strong males, preferably football players, to push Herb through his walking paces as he himself had done. Athletes, he felt, would be strong enough to impose the rigorous physical discipline his father needed. Apparently, the young men Steve visualized were otherwise engaged. Calls to area colleges failed to yield even a single response until Anna, then in her first year of graduate work in physical therapy, responded. Anna, a statuesque blond, blue-eyed young woman worked with Herb in a two-hour session each weekend until her graduation almost two years later, focusing on his frozen hand and arm.

Additional Support

But I also wanted additional support to walk Herb around the house in repetitions and motivate him to do his chair exercises. Recognizing that it was easier to work with people I knew and trusted, I called in my personal trainer, whom I'd known for almost four years prior to Herb's stroke. I worked out with Deborah several morning sessions each week and was grateful that she, too, was eager to join our team.

Deborah and Sara trained with the outpatient PT at Metro to administer bed, chair, and transfer exercises as well as the proper walking gait. Both learned how to stretch Herb's right arm and clawlike hand. His nonfunctioning fingers were curled tightly into a fist. Sara became skilled at using an electric stimulator on Herb's arm muscles in an effort to relax the lower arm and fingers.

We added another member to the roster, a tai chi instructor trained in northern China and willing to offer his hard stomach for a punch from any nonbeliever. Several times in that first year John Lee was ready to cancel our in-home sessions because he felt Herb did not take the instruction seriously or practice sufficiently. Tai chi is an act of faith. Herb lacked that faith. The underlying principle of the exercise is that if you think positive thoughts you can accomplish whatever goals you set. Herb somehow scraped up a little more conviction and continues with tai chi twice a week.

I felt the claims John made were unbelievable, more oriented to someone with a mystical background. Tai chi required putting aside my training in science and engineering. Could I do this? Did I even want to try?

An Unbalanced Relationship

We had a strange imbalance. When other people like Sara, Otis, and John were around, Herb would joke and banter a little with them. With me he was usually grumpy, selfish, irritable, and silent. His responses were in his facial changes. When he wanted something he would point; his urinal request was a grunt; and when he wanted to be alone, he would wave me away. I felt as though I was living with Harpo Marx, but without the warmth and humor.

Dinner became a trying ritual. Herb's glucose testing and medications came first, followed by soup and a hot entrée. He began eating before I sat down and then looked to me as an audience for his discomfort. I placed a newspaper between the two of us so that I did not have to see his unhappy grimacing. *I tried not to look at Herb while I ate. But I chose not to move my plate into another room and break off all contact.*

Of all my caregiving responsibilities, managing his difficult behavior in the early months at home was the toughest. Why, I repeatedly asked our psychologist,[24] does he communicate with others and ignore me? I was the one shouldering the heaviest responsibilities, turning my life inside out to care for him and feeling more like a drudge with each passing day. *I missed my husband and especially missed the emotional closeness we had shared for so many years. The loneliness was overwhelming.* This theme recurred in our many sessions. Of all of the challenges in my role of caregiver, this emotional imbalance was the toughest to overcome.

It's true. I guess it was the old bromide of hurting the one you most love. And I wanted to inflict pain.

Fear of Falling

A stroke survivor's instability in standing, fragility in falling, and inability to break a fall creates an ever-present hazard. A friend's mother repeatedly called 911 when her husband fell in their apartment and she couldn't lift him. I worried about what I would do if that happened when Herb and I were alone. A 150-pound sack of dead weight is a tremendous strain, and I worried that I could pull my back, or worse. An incapacitating injury to me as caregiver was unthinkable.

The first fall came when Herb tried to lift himself to a sitting position at the edge of the bed to use the plastic urinal. Although the hospital bed had safety guards on both sides, Herb was once again sleeping in our king-size bed[25] and lacked that protection. I tried tucking the sheeting tightly under the mattress to secure him in place, but he pulled it out. In the middle of the night I heard a thump. There he was, splayed on the floor. The first time, Steve was home and lifted him back onto the bed. The second time, my brother-in-law was visiting and made the transfer. This time we were on our own.

Steve recognized the need before leaving and had designed and constructed a low table with a side handle as an intermediate step for lifting. The sturdy, broad-based device served as an intermediate vertical stop. While Herb held on to the steel post on his left side, I folded his sprawled right leg at the

---

[24] *Dr. Dreben, with Herb's permission, conducts shared sessions for us, which, while geared to Herb, are very helpful for both of us.*

[25] *The hospital bed, now a permanent fixture in Steve's old room, provides backup for Herb should he become ill or require extra support.*

knee; then he pushed down and I lifted. By working together we could raise him up about a foot. It wasn't easy, it wasn't smooth, but it worked. We had various occasions in the next few months to rely on that low table. It is still in a corner of our living room.

Steve was very talented with coming up with nonstandard solutions to our problems. He simply recognized a void and off he went. Invariably he was successful. He was unconventional yet highly effective.

What Next?

Trying to plan for the future in this strange, new, upside-down, wheelchair-circumscribed world seemed like a Herculean feat, compounded by the effort of putting back together the pieces of my own shattered emotional well-being. My job was to make the recovery program fall into place somehow. *I would simply have to deal with my caregiver woes at another time.* The combined effort was not going to be easy, but I felt that we would find our way forward.

Lessons Learned

Planning routine respite care is essential.

Fatigue makes caregivers grumpy. It can also lower resistance and make you ill. Make time to rest during the day and at night. You can't problem solve and keep things in perspective when you are tired and feel backed into a corner. Ask friends for referrals to qualified caregivers. Recommendations and referrals from friends are more credible than agencies or a blind ad in the newspaper. Above all, check multiple references carefully.

Train people whom you already know and trust.

Seek people who are bright, enthusiastic, and strong enough to handle the transitioning and pivoting required by a partially or fully disabled survivor. Ask your outpatient physical therapist to train your team in proper gait techniques and exercises.

Establish a schedule.

Consistency and regularity help you gain better control of a difficult situation. Few days at the beginning will go the way you've planned, but a format helps both caregiver and survivor adapt more easily to the routine and home life.

Discourage casual drop-in visitors.

At the beginning the caregiver has a hectic pace, which is best maintained without the distraction of unscheduled company. Caregivers as well as survivors need downtime and a few treasured corners for retreat, without demands or interruptions, especially in the early weeks.

Join a caregiver support group.

Spend time with others in similar situations. Contact the social worker at your hospital to find out about possible groups meeting in your area. Some of these groups also have a simultaneous but separate group meeting for stroke survivors.

Prepare for falls.

Poor balance leads to falls. Few people have the strength to lift a partially paralyzed stroke survivor. Plan in advance. Consider a low bench with a handle positioned on the working side as an in-between step in maneuvering your patient back into bed or wheelchair. It may take time but is preferable to calling EMS.

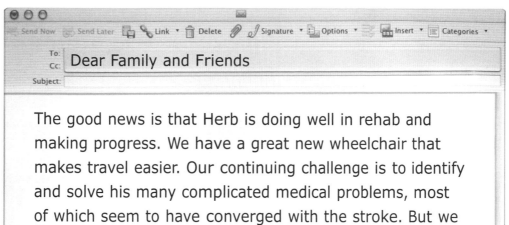

The good news is that Herb is doing well in rehab and making progress. We have a great new wheelchair that makes travel easier. Our continuing challenge is to identify and solve his many complicated medical problems, most of which seem to have converged with the stroke. But we keep working on them, one at a time. Keep your fingers crossed.

B

CHAPTER 7
Medical Complications

When You Think Things Can't Get Any Worse, They Do

Overwhelmed by a difficult adjustment to the 24/7 caregiving routine, I had little time or inclination to research anything but the most pressing information about stroke and its effects. The general statistics I found were sobering. Of an estimated 730,000 Americans who have a first stroke, 5 to 14 percent will have a second within one year. Even worse, 24 percent of women and 42 percent of men have a second or third stroke within the first five years. Herb was a ready candidate with a neon sign. As a male with preexisting diabetes, his risk was two and a half times higher than for nondiabetic survivors.

Lowering the Risk of Another Stroke

The campaign to save my husband's life was fearsome. I focused on factors that could quickly and effectively minimize his risk for another stroke. These included improving his eating and exercising patterns, and actively identifying medical problems before they became emergencies.

The hospital info packs offered me little beyond basic symptoms and causes. Only more recent Internet searches for "stroke complications," rather than for just "stroke," have yielded links to other varied problems Herb has experienced. These include constipation, retention of urine and urinary tract infections, depression, sleep apnea, and chronic pain.[26] *On my own, I tackled each problem in turn, determined to solve our medical jigsaw puzzle but lacking most of the pieces to put it all together. An understanding that most of Herb's lingering problems stemmed directly from the stroke and might lessen over time could have saved many sleepless nights and tears.*

Herb had these complications and more. In addition to a preexisting but misdiagnosed heart condition, he also developed a vision-threatening side effect from one of his medications. Complex problems, one after the other and most within the span of the first three years, challenged my faith in Herb's recovery and myself. *Often I felt as though we were white-water rafting by ourselves without oars.*

Nothing Is Routine

Frequent medical appointments with numerous specialists, including rehab, internal medicine, neurologist, neurological interventionist, urologist, and psychologist continued for most of the first three years.

Because of the precariousness of his situation, Herb often had multiple weekly appointments. Scheduling was generally imposed on us and often conflicted with therapies at MetroHealth Center for Rehabilitation across town. Our internist monitored his progress; the neurological interventionist ran frequent brain scans; the rehab specialist supervised recovery and therapies; the urologist tried to eradicate a persistent urinary tract infection; and the rehab psychologist tried to scoop up emotional fragments.

---

[26] *V.S. Doshi and others, "Complications in Stroke Patients: A Study Carried Out at the Rehabilitation Medicine Service, Changi General Hospital," Singapore Medical Journal 44, no. 12 (2003): 643–652.*

Each problem generated more specialists and more appointments. Sometimes treatment for one problem led to a new series of interventions. For example, Cipro, a very strong antibiotic prescribed to combat Herb's urinary infection, required frequent monitoring with blood tests, urine specimens, and follow-up appointments. A diagnosis of iron deficiency anemia required thirteen weekly injections in addition to repeated lab analysis.

Diabetes 2

Diabetes, which began long before Herb's stroke and may have precipitated its onset,[27] turned out to be the easiest problem to address.

Herb never made much of an issue of his late-onset, noninsulin-dependent diabetes despite the fact that it ran in his family. Prestroke, although he monitored his glucose level several times a week, he didn't view it as a big deal. Poststroke, his high glucose level became my responsibility. I carefully recorded readings twice a day. Through medication, exercise, and diet, his levels almost immediately came under control. Results from a quarterly hemoglobin A1c blood test indicate steady readings of below 6.0, well within normal bounds (see Chapter 12, *Food-Smart Recovery*).

I continue to keep records in a medical loose-leaf folder, divided by sections, so that I can monitor patterns and adjust medications as necessary. Herb had difficulty accepting the direct correlation between certain foods and blood sugar. *It took time and patience to demonstrate that an ice cream cone or piece of chocolate cake can raise his glucose level as many as fifty points during monitoring some three or four hours later. His food preferences and erratic eating patterns still cause dissension.*

Missed Cardiac Diagnosis

Herb's mysterious left arm pain continued after the stroke and was particularly troubling during various therapies. Hot and cold packs brought no relief. With a nagging sense of unease, I requested an emergency appointment with our internist. Still unable to identify the source of the pain, he prescribed nitroglycerin as a precaution.

---

[27] *Diabetes is considered as a possible precursor to stroke.*

In mid-March 2002, several months short of the first anniversary of his stroke and after four years of complaints, Herb awoke one morning complaining again of left arm pain. Since he was still in bed, it obviously was not exertion-related. Nitroglycerin prescribed as a safety factor worked within minutes, much faster than Advil and other pain relievers I'd previously used. Nitro's speed and effectiveness in calming the spasm indicated a strong connection with his heart.

The cardiologist suspected arterial blockage and strongly recommended that Herb undergo angioplasty[28] that following Monday morning, three days later. Our daughter Kathryn flew in to be with us. She and I kissed Herb and wished him good luck. Then we sat in the patients' waiting room, a comfortable area with couches, tables, and even a hot chocolate dispenser. I carried the standard two-pound bag of M&M's in my backpack.

An hour or so later, the cardiologist came out and sat down with us, saying that he had sobering news: Herb was almost 100 percent blocked in one coronary artery, 95 percent in another, and a third blockage had formed an alternate routing, which seemed to have saved his life. The doctor recommended immediate quintuple bypass surgery. Hearing ringing alarms, he rushed back. Herb was suffering anginal pain[29] on the table.

Now with no time for bypass surgery, the cardiologist inserted two stents to open the blocked arteries, and Herb remained hospitalized overnight. Kathryn flew home to her family. I again sat upright on a hard chair in the hospital room, wrapped in a blanket, and monitored his breathing through the night.

Later the cardiologist told us that Herb would probably suffer a heart attack by June, in fewer than three months, and require bypass surgery then. I questioned why we had to passively wait for this heart attack. Somehow, with Herb's history of stroke and diabetes, the prospect of further surgery seemed terribly risky to me. A wait of another two months in limbo was even more alarming. A second specialist within the hospital corroborated the first doctor's recommendation.

---

[28] *Cardiac angioplasty is similar to brain angioplasty and is considered less invasive than bypass surgery. It requires a small slit in the groin, then sliding a balloon into the artery, as opposed to cracking open the chest.*

[29] *Angina, a symptom of coronary artery disease (CAD), occurs when the heart muscle does not get enough blood flow. This decreases the oxygen supply to the heart muscle and presents an emergency situation. The blood flow must be immediately reestablished.*

My sister-in-law, Lois, arranged an immediate consultation with Dr. Miriam Cohen, an eminent diagnostician and chief of cardiology at Union Memorial Hospital in Baltimore, and we drove down there.

After a comprehensive battery of tests, including nuclear stress, EKG, cardiac photography, and detailed blood analysis, Dr. Cohen reassured us that there was no reason to perform quintuple bypass surgery at this time. Herb's stents were functioning properly, and surgery for Herb as a diabetic stroke survivor would be very risky. More to the point, she found serious factors complicating his recovery, namely critical iron deficiency anemia and a dangerously elevated white cell count, the latter possibly related to a persistent urological infection. She urged that Herb have several blood transfusions immediately on our return to Cleveland and see his urologist and gastroenterologist to determine the sources of infection and blood loss. Her bottom line was that Herb must be medically managed more closely.

We trust Dr. Cohen and believe it is well worth the six-hour drive to Baltimore every six months for an appointment. Based on her recommendation, we identified a local cardiologist willing to work with her in an emergency. The results are stunning. Recent nuclear stress tests indicate that Herb's heart is stronger and pumping more evenly than before his stroke. He has also regained facial color and much of his former strength.

Depression

From the beginning Herb's moods became increasingly morose and tearful. Often he expressed feelings of worthlessness and powerlessness, yet did little to help himself. The continuous cycle of depression limited his improvement. Sometimes he would beg me to put him into a nursing home.

Depression is a medical condition that results from abnormal functioning of the brain, although episodes can also be triggered by stress, side effects from medications, and other factors not necessarily related to stroke. The average duration of major depression in poststroke survivors is just under a year. Herb's has lasted more than three years.

His bouts with depression began long before the stroke, but now he experienced roller-coaster gyrations, and the downs lasted longer than any he'd had before. We addressed our joint frustrations in monthly sessions with Herb's rehab psychologist. Discussions ranged from his perceived powerlessness to sexual dysfunction. Celexa, an antidepressant prescribed by his internist, helped, but resolution has been very slow.

Constipation and Urinary Tract Problems

Constipation is the most common complication among stroke survivors. Among the many causes are the stroke event itself, immobility after stroke, and dehydration. Chronic constipation is also a mood-altering problem. We began with oral laxatives and enemas, but Herb found more continuous regularity through a daily combination of MiraLax, a prescription powder recommended by our gastroenterologist, and Citrucel, buttressed by periodic doses of milk of magnesia.

Herb's urinary frequency and incontinence primarily result from a combination of factors, including inpatient catheterization,[30] the stroke event itself, constant sitting in the wheelchair, and an enlarged prostate. A continuing challenge (see Chapter 13, *Toileting Nightmares*), improvement does come gradually. For most of the first two-plus years, he used four to six urinals nightly. Not much of a water drinker to begin with, he refused most fluids, especially with his dinner, hoping that this limitation would help him sleep through the night. It only made the constipation worse.

Sleep Apnea

Herb complained about not sleeping through the night almost immediately after the stroke. Physicians prescribed sleeping pills but none worked. In addition to varied prescriptions, I tried over-the-counter Tylenol and Tylenol PM, but still Herb yearned for a full, refreshing night's sleep. He felt tired, weak, and irritable.

After the first month, he begged to move back into our master bedroom and king-size bed. He said he felt isolated in the hospital bed and thought the

---

[30] *Catheterization is the procedure of inserting a tube (catheter) through the urethra into the bladder to remove urine.*

change would help him sleep better. *I was confused about what I wanted. In many ways it was a relief to tuck Herb into bed and reserve an extra few hours for myself reading, watching television, even sleeping in snatches before interruption. I also preferred distance from the ubiquitous urinal, worried that it could spill all over our more expensive mattress. Yet I understood his need for intimacy and how it might improve his sleep.*

We made the move, and now it was my turn to lie awake and be sleep deprived. His snoring was louder and odder than prestroke because it would suddenly and abruptly break off in the middle. More than once I counted to forty before he resumed breathing. Still Herb claimed he didn't sleep at all and was as tired in the morning as the night before. The sleep problem rippled through his daytime activity as he became increasingly depressed and lacked energy to tackle his therapies.

Our hospital has a sleep apnea lab. That was the upside. The downside was that demand was so heavy it took many months to get an appointment. Herb's sleep test was in early March, three months after we initiated a request with our internist.

The sleeping area itself resembled a typical motel room except that it was rimmed by high-tech equipment. Electrodes planted all over Herb's scalp, cheeks, chin, chest, and legs made him look like Hollywood's version of a space alien. Data from brain waves, heart rhythm, eye movements, breathing, and snores were fed by cable into a computer center down the hall, where sleep disorder specialists monitored it for sleep patterns, stages, and cycles. In spite of all of these disturbances, Herb slept. *Obviously, I didn't. The room was noisy, the bed was hard, and I worried about driving home at 5:00 a.m. in a heavy snowstorm after we were discharged from the sleep lab.*

The assessment was not a surprise. Herb did have sleep apnea. His treatment required sleeping with a scuba-type mask fed by a super loud breathing machine. Positioned by his bedside, this compact "lung" fed oxygen to supposedly improve his sleep efficiency. The specialists told us it might take Herb several weeks to adjust. Not so. The first machine lasted under fifteen minutes. He discarded several more during abortive trials with other systems in even less time and refused all further sleep support. Relieved not to have any encumbrances, he has slumbered well ever since. *Needless to say, I didn't pine for the lost machines, which I could hear even when I slept in the abandoned hospital bed down the hall, wearing my earplugs.*

I found this entire experience frustrating. Because the apnea test is a long one, we felt it would merit a lengthy analysis. However, after waiting almost three hours, the specialist treated us in summary fashion. He made a cursory recommendation that took maybe five minutes, refused to answer our questions, and then left.

Facial Pain

A small percentage of stroke survivors develop nerve pain. The onset of pain may occur with the stroke or several months afterward. Herb's pain arose just over a year later.

Located in the right cheek area just above the corner of his upper lip, this throbbing ache came on suddenly. Pain sometimes reached 6 to 8 out of 10 on the standard pain scale. Exercise, eating, speaking, and stress intensified the pain, leaving Herb depressed, uncooperative, and dysfunctional. Often he sat at the kitchen table, head in hands and tears flowing.

Over a two-year period, we sought help from a variety of specialists, advancing through five neurologists, a pain center, and a facial therapist. We also went to a consultant in craniofacial pain and jaw dysfunctions, who developed a splint to prevent Herb from grinding his teeth. Special painkillers, nerve blocks, medications developed for epilepsy and depression, acupuncture, and relaxation-distraction exercises had no effect.

Finally a neurovascular surgeon specializing in deep brain stimulation identified the precise cause of Herb's pain as damage to the thalamus from the stroke. Rather than invasively control the pain through major cranial surgery, I turned back to our internist and in desperation asked for just plain-vanilla pain medication.[31] Used sparingly, it brought some relief. Finally.

---

[31] *Tramadol HCl is considerably more effective in quelling Herb's facial pain than the very expensive Neurontin, which did nothing.*

No solution is apparent, and this pain is truly a curse. The symptoms amplify with any form of strenuous activity. Most recently it shows up as I exercise. The pain pill helps somewhat, but I don't like relying on it. Many of the treatments prescribed were useless, more to provide answers for something they didn't know how to treat.

After two very rocky years, the pain has lessened somewhat. Whether we can attribute improvement to one or a combination of all of the many measures makes little difference. Perhaps Herb's brain just needed more time to heal. *While waging this enormous battle to help Herb survive his acute stroke, it was mind-boggling that something from left field could threaten our efforts and almost destroy both of us. Were it not for this pain, I believe Herb could have accomplished much more, much faster.*

Complications from Medication

Pharmaceuticals have side effects. We carry an updated list of all medications to each appointment. At home I crosscheck new prescriptions with a *Physicians' Desk Reference* book. We've learned that no one physician, including our internist, can take time to monitor each drug's interaction with the rest. With so many specialists and pharmaceuticals for so many complicated problems, dangerous side effects sneak through. We have had several bad experiences.

The worst instance was when Herb complained about a film over his right eye. He experienced no discomfort, but his sight was blurry in the morning, improving toward the end of the day. Following a number of tests, we learned that Herb had acute glaucoma. Blocked vessels in his right eye were rapidly building pressure and, if not immediately relieved, could lead to permanent blindness within hours. Our ophthalmologist performed laser surgery, making a small hole in the upper left area of the pupil to relieve the pressure and save Herb's vision.

The physician later asked about any new medications we had added since Herb's last checkup three months before. I mentioned a long-acting medication prescribed for urinary frequency. "That could do it," he said. Our urologist concurred with the assessment and told us to halt the medication immediately. Although instructions on the packaging warned against usage by patients with glaucoma, that caveat did not previously apply.

Working through the wide range of complexities and potentially adverse drug interactions, we remain ever vigilant for symptoms tied to the introduction of new medications. Our medical complications are rivaled in intensity only by the challenges of seeking help within the medical system.

Lessons Learned

Choose your physicians carefully.

Everyone needs an internist or primary care physician even without an emergency. Choose your physicians with care. Research (you may even Google on the Internet) your doctors and their histories, how they practice, and whether they have any malpractice suits pending. Look for training (board certification is a plus), referral by physicians whom you trust, willingness to manage your case, and an ability to communicate well. Find out how to alert your doctors when you have a serious problem and require prompt response. Then put them to the test: if your physician is too busy to listen to your problems (be concise and prioritize the most severe first!), find one who will. Ask your doctor[32] to review all your medications for problem interactions and continuing relevance.

Insist your physicians use understandable words and descriptions.

Physician-speak is a language that laypeople do not understand. As patients we find medical terms far beyond our capabilities and training. While many courts provide translators for the adjudicated, medical systems do not. Insist that your physicians answer your questions and provide descriptions and instructions in everyday, understandable language. Raise questions and concerns. If you don't understand an instruction or explanation, ask again. You have a right to know. Conversely, if your first language is not English and you have problems understanding what your

---

[32] *We require oversight by our internist because we live in an age where the high cost of pharmaceuticals is a big issue. I purchase from a number of different pharmacies, including a Canadian source.*

doctor is saying (or your doctor has problems understanding you), bring a translator with you so that there will be no misunderstandings on either side about this important information.

Recognize that stroke can precipitate many other conditions.

Often you may feel confused by many interlocking medical problems, each one treated in isolation. Question your rehab specialist or internist about a possible interaction between stroke and complications manifested by your survivor. You shouldn't have to figure this out on your own. Recovery takes time.

Research stroke complications.

Many of the complications affecting your stroke survivor may result from the overall brain injury. Although you may require multiple specialists, insist that your internist coordinate this treatment. Integrated teamwork, still unknown in many tertiary care facilities, is a very effective approach because it treats the entire patient rather than isolated parts. Pain, just one possible complication, affects 5 percent of stroke survivors and often occurs at the time of stroke or even a year later. Twenty percent of patients improve over a period of years.[33]

Research stroke complications on your own using the Internet, available in most libraries, and a search engine such as Google. Identify medical Web sites that discuss stroke complications using keywords: *stroke complications, stroke,* and *stroke rehabilitation.* Your survivor may have one or more of these problems or none, but at least you will know how to track them and respond should any develop.

Consult with another specialist, preferably one outside your medical system.

Should you question specific aspects of the survivor's medical condition, treatment, or surgical recommendations, consult with a qualified specialist

---

[33] *"Chronic Pain After Stroke": http://www.painrelieffoundation.org.uk*

who is preferably board certified and located in a system unrelated to your current hospital and physicians. Arrange for the transfer of pertinent records for review or carry them yourself, an excellent way to make sure they arrive on time. Most insurance plans cover a second opinion. In case of doubt, you should consider a third opinion.

Accept ultimate responsibility for managing your survivor's condition.

Today the caregiver or chosen advocate must take command. The doctor-patient relationship has changed: time slots are limited, appointments require long waiting periods, and overscheduled physicians have too little time to troubleshoot. Report unusual patterns and problems. Make your communications clear and concise.

Write questions and concerns down on paper before each medical appointment.

An appointment forces you to think through your priorities. Organize and write down questions, problems, and changes in medications in advance so that you allow more time for targeted discussion.

Participate in all decisions about your stroke survivor's treatment.

You and your physician should agree on exactly what will be done during each step of your survivor's care. Know who will be treating your patient, how long the treatment will last, and what a new test or medication is likely to achieve.

Take notes and follow instructions.

Carry a pen and pad, and write down all instructions and recommendations. If your doctor calls for significant changes, repeat them to assure accuracy. If you have any question about instructions or find unexpected results or problems, contact your physician immediately.

Maintain your own medical records.

Request copies of reports from all specialists on your medical team. Assume that exchange among and within health care institutions carries a long lag time. Your information will fill the gap. Keep a loose-leaf binder with separate sections for each medical problem. File and date copies of reports, discharge summaries, tests, and lists of medications in corresponding sections, beginning with the most recent report first. Carry the binder with you when you travel, begin new therapy programs, or add new specialists to your medical roster.

Organize pharmaceutical records.

List each medication, dosage, quantity, time of day, and prescribing physician. Include over-the-counter products. A word processor will make it easier to store and update easily. Bring a current list to each medical and dental appointment (see Appendix E).

Create a supermap for medications.

A medication map covers your entire day's scheduling. It plots when you give which medications, the dosage, and any other key information, including the name of the physician prescribing the medication and the date of the initial prescription. At one glance, the sheet will tell you what, when, and how much. Time slots on your map should correspond with those on your medicine pillbox (see Appendix C).

Bring an updated list of medications to each medical and dental visit.

The realistic potential for side effects and drug interactions requires constant review. Know the medications your stroke survivor takes and why he/she takes them. Provide an updated list of medications and corresponding dosages at each appointment. Update all information regularly. A simple sheet of paper, its information preferably stored on a word processor, is much more efficient than trying to memorize complex names randomly or carrying bags of prescription bottles.

Arrange a separate place or box to store medications.

A self-contained plastic pillbox is ideal. List by order of the day to correspond with your medication map. Also keep a pad where you store your medications so that you can write down any questions or problems for discussion at your next appointment.

Watch for harmful side effects.

Read pharmaceutical information on labels and enclosed instructions for usage directions and possible side effects (called PPIs, for Patient Prescription Information).[34] Remain vigilant for symptoms associated with a new prescription. Some side effects that occur rarely may not be listed. Should something unusual but minor occur, monitor the problem and report it to your physician. If the problem is acute, such as blurry vision, contact your ophthalmologist, and/or internist, immediately.

---

[34] *Unfortunately, pharmaceutical instructions and warnings are in small type and difficult both to read and understand. If in doubt, question your pharmacist.*

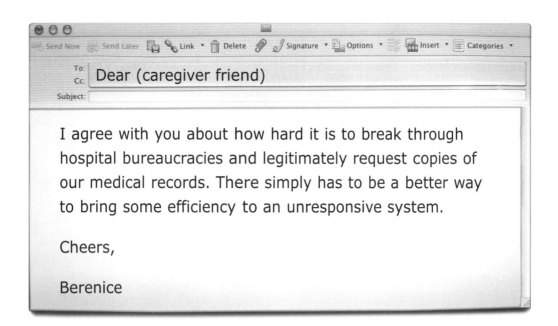

Dear (caregiver friend)

I agree with you about how hard it is to break through hospital bureaucracies and legitimately request copies of our medical records. There simply has to be a better way to bring some efficiency to an unresponsive system.

Cheers,

Berenice

CHAPTER 8
Maneuvering through the Medical Maze

A Crash Course in Working through a Medical Bureaucracy

Each appointment involves long runs through endless hospital corridors preceded by frantic searches in the parking garage to find a handicapped parking spot wide enough to transition Herb to his wheelchair. Most of our visits are with specialists located in the same building and often on adjacent floors of a vast medical complex. In the first three years, we requested but received few opportunities to bundle appointments and tests for the same day or, even better, the same part of the day.

Timely Medical Appointments Are an Oxymoron

From the beginning we had many appointments for Herb's wide range of complications. Each required a frantic rush to get to the medical complex on time followed by an additional one to three hours in a crowded waiting room, leaving us to wonder why the wait for a regularly scheduled appointment took so long.

During extended lulls I usually raced to the cafeteria to bring back a sandwich for Herb. As a diabetic he had to eat regularly. *Devaluing the patient's time in long waits still angers and frustrates me. A medical emergency is understandable, but a continuing pattern is unforgivable. Although some patients require more time than others, and we certainly do, that time should be built into the system.*

We recognize some waiting is necessary and bring along books to read. But two- or three-hour waits must be eliminated—or at least reduced. There has to be a better approach to this dehumanizing system.

Finding a Case Manager

Dr. Felver, our internist and good friend, was often called out of the country for frequent medical trips to the United Arab Emirates and was not readily accessible for our continued, complex needs. I reluctantly informed him of our decision to change physicians. Based on personal and medical recommendations, we met with Dr. Alan Weiss, within the same hospital system, who had coincidently attended both high school and college with our daughter Miriam. Dr. Weiss assured us he would handle Herb's difficult and time-consuming management task. Moreover, he agreed to e-mail as a fast and efficient mechanism for mutual communication when I had troubling questions and problems.

Too Many Specialists, Too Little Coordination

We now had about twenty specialists. Each worked in a vacuum, oblivious to Herb's other medical problems. Few seemed to exchange information or review records with others of our team. I was incredulous about this seeming indifference and kept asking myself: How can this be possible? *Why don't they share records and treat the patient as a whole being rather than just parts? Who puts it all together?*

For almost an entire week following our first trip to Baltimore, I had a recurring nightmare in which I find myself pushing Herb's wheelchair along an endless corridor. *Closed examination rooms flank me on both sides. Outside each door stands a specialist wearing a colorful, plumed mask. With a wide sweep of his arms, each one beckons us in. I don't know whom to trust or which room to enter. But I know I must choose correctly because my decision means life or death for my husband.*

After many upsetting nights, I awoke with the solution. Herb and I were professional communicators. Our clients paid us to sort through disparate elements to identify and communicate their strategic common denominator. Why couldn't I just apply that skill to this situation?

I faxed an identical memo to all of our specialists. It identified everyone on Herb's medical team by name, specialty, and telephone and fax numbers. The memo summarized significant developments over the previous two weeks, listed current medications, and introduced Herb's new internist–case manager. I explicitly requested that all future reports be sent to our internist, cardiologist, and me. No exceptions.

Lassoing the Medical Bureaucracy

Medical institutions are huge bureaucracies that are neither patient nor friendly. Herb is fortunate to have a well-qualified and responsive medical team, but this formative process has not been easy. Our team, which crosses two states and four hospital systems, includes physicians who go out of their way, sometimes on their own time, to follow up Herb's case, and the majority have responded to us quickly in our times of need.

But it is not easy to find responsive medical professionals who treat us with dignity and respect. Sometimes it requires a lot of searching and a well-timed referral. For example, rigorous walking on his braces irritated the bottoms of Herb's feet, a dangerous problem for a diabetic. We went through a variety of specialists within our hospital system seeking help: podiatrist, vascular specialist, brace specialist, even a shoe specialist. Each tedious appointment required slight modifications to the braces with multiple follow-ups. Still his redness and irritation worsened.

Then Sara made a profound suggestion. She recommended a podiatric physician and surgeon in independent practice on the city's west side, who was excellent. He agreed to see us the same day.

This podiatric specialist, a marathon runner himself, examined Herb's feet, braces, and shoes. He then left the room with braces and shoes in hand, and retreated to the next room. There, while we waited, he made the modifications, filing off rough edges from the bottom of the braces and opening a seam at the front side of Herb's right shoe. No fuss, no follow-ups or stretched-out appointments, referrals, or added equipment. Then he helped us down a temporary plywood ramp and back to our car.

He is a good guy. Without pomp or ceremony he got the job done.

We have also experienced a number of specialists who are themselves legends in their own minds. My job is to weed them out as quickly as possible. One particularly flagrant example involved a specialist in the lipid area, who came highly recommended. Our internist said he would initiate the appointment. One week later I received a call from an inarticulate female voice about a medical appointment. I recognized the name of our hospital system but could not make out either the doctor or specialty she was calling about. She arbitrarily gave Herb a 6:00 p.m. appointment the following week. We already had a 10:00 a.m. appointment scheduled for the same campus on the same day, along with several other appointments on different days that week. I explained our circumstances and the difficulty of multiple trips on one day for my wheelchair-bound husband. Her retort was: "Take it or leave it." I gladly declined.

Later that evening a message on our answering machine awaited us from Dr. ——, telling Herb that his wife had behaved badly. This physician said we should consider ourselves fortunate he would even agree to an appointment. Needless to say, we did not return his call and easily found another lipid specialist.

All Things Considered

All things considered, we value and appreciate the outstanding physicians on our team, both professionally and personally. In addition to their professional expertise, a number of them continue to offer us thoughtful and compassionate support. We sometimes meet young residents on the medical campus from the original neurological team when Herb was first hospitalized. Several still stop us and offer encouragement. We have hope that these residents will develop into well-rounded, responsive specialists.

Lessons Learned

Coordinate diverse specialists.

Cooperation with your internist–case manager and diverse team, especially in a complicated case, is vital. You may have to initiate this communication by providing a composite list of all your specialists' names and addresses. Should you feel your specialists do not exchange pertinent information in a timely and helpful manner or that they treat your request brusquely, replace an uncooperative physician with one who will work with you (see Appendix F for a sample summary sheet.)

Recognize your responsibility to share timely information.

The patient's advocate has a responsibility to share information, arrive on time for appointments, and bring questions, observations, and updated records from outside consults. However, be judicious and work through your questions and problems in advance so that you do not take advantage of the physician's time.

Follow treatment directions.

You have a responsibility to follow treatment directions. Write these down during the medical appointment. Arrange follow-up appointments on a regular basis. Request extra appointments only when absolutely urgent.

Also check whether your internist and/or rehab specialist accept e-mail as a means for communicating perplexing questions. Although it may lack the immediacy of a telephone call, the Internet promotes an exchange of communications while minimizing unnecessary medical appointments and telephone calls.

Bundle appointments.

It is fatiguing for patient and caregiver, especially one with walker or wheelchair, to be forced repeatedly into a series of separate appointments on separate days within the same complex. Ask the appointment scheduler[35] to bundle two or more appointments on the same day. If your request is denied, appeal to a supervisor.

Organize and maintain a business card list of your physicians.

Organized information is vital in an emergency. Request business cards from each doctor and anyone on the doctor's staff you might need to speak with, and store them alphabetically in a special business card file. The plastic sleeves allow flexibility for rearranging information. As an alternative, wrap a rubber band around the pile of cards. Each card should include printed name, address, medical specialty, telephone and fax number, and an optional e-mail address. For fast, easy reference, list your patient's hospital identification number and copies of insurance and supplementary insurance cards in the top sleeve of the organizer.

Break through the telephone logjam when you have a serious medical need.

Medical offices are notorious for long telephone waits. State your serious need and ask for immediate help at the beginning of your phone comments. Otherwise yours will not stand out from the many calls in the office queue.

---

[35] *The Cleveland Clinic has a battery of schedulers associated with each department and charged with the task of scheduling available appointments. Sometimes they inform the patient after the arrangements are made.*

You can appeal poor or indifferent treatment.

Assuming you have unsuccessfully tried all available means to contact your physician with legitimate concerns, to organize appointments, or to request copies of medical records, several recourses remain open. First, request help from your hospital's ombudsperson. Next, contact your hospital system's chief executive officer (through the main number). The person who takes your call can usually direct you to the proper channel for resolution. If still unsuccessful, assuming you have a choice, switch to another health care system.

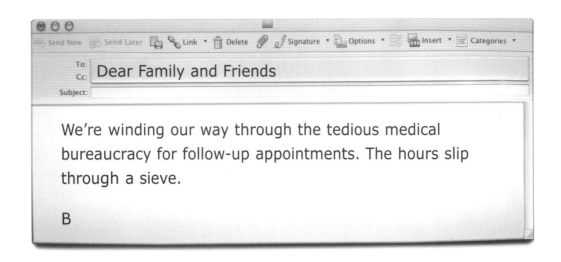

We're winding our way through the tedious medical bureaucracy for follow-up appointments. The hours slip through a sieve.

B

CHAPTER 9
Caregiver's Anger
Anger Management Is an Oxymoron

The literature attributes caregiver anger to the "condition," a euphemism for the stroke that "happened to both of us." But reading about it didn't relieve my sometimes hostile and aggressive moods. I struggled not to unload these feelings on Herb, though they hovered just beneath the surface.

Targeted Anger

I was angry with the Cleveland Clinic for allowing "a small stroke in a prime area of real estate" to become a massive wipeout. I was angry they understaffed their emergency room. And I was angry they failed to identify Herb's rapid deterioration as he lay hooked to sophisticated monitors in the neurological unit. I was angry at MetroHealth Medical Center for indifferent nursing and ineptitude. And I was deeply angry at Herb for his casual acceptance of diabetes and corresponding risks prior to the stroke. At the bottom of it all, I blamed him and deeply resented the passive-aggressive mode he would often slip into, refusing to help himself as though he thought all of this was my fault. Mutual self-pity threatened to defeat both of us. *His frequent regressions and sick-chicken appearance—closed eyes, slackened jaws, and huddled shoulders—drove me to question why I was battling so hard.*

I desperately missed our former life. With our children grown up and massive family and financial responsibilities for colleges and weddings behind us, our business had permitted time for trips around the world and fascinating seminars at area universities. The stroke terminated these pleasures. My life became a nonstop race from one hospital and treatment program to another.

But maybe I was angriest with myself for not kicking open the doors of the Cleveland Clinic three years before the stroke and demanding a logical reason for Herb's persistent left arm pain. I should have sought an outside consult much earlier. I acquiesced and was wrong. I was also troubled that I had chosen not to remain in Canada to seek immediate help from the community hospital. *As it turned out, since we were well beyond that initial three-hour lead, the Clinic was the best place for Herb. But still doubts and guilt nibbled away my confidence, and I replayed this decision repeatedly.*

My thoughts sometimes return to Ellie, our first home social worker, and her "go with the flow" advice that drove me up the wall. I now understand her concerns for my mental and physical health. But my fight for life and recovery is immediate and broader. Much of it involves making order out of chaos.

Sometimes in anger I kick open doors that won't budge with gentle knocking. During Herb's first two years following the stroke, my blood pressure rose from a prestroke high of about 130/80 to peaks of 180/112. *The long periods in the waiting rooms were the worst. I could feel my head pounding and blood pressure rising in spontaneous reaction to too many physicians and their often indifferent staffs.*

It took a long time for my blood pressure to ratchet down to manageable range. As a stress release, I turned to blacktopping our long driveway. It felt good to swish around black asphalt and to be alone for four uninterrupted hours. Each can of asphalt had a physician's name on it. When I total the cost of materials and what I paid for someone else to watch my husband, actual savings over a blacktop company were not that great. However, by factoring in savings from professional fees for a psychologist or psychiatrist, I think I came out ahead.

As for me, the "why me?" was always there. To live a full life prestroke and then, with no forewarning, be dumbstruck at the severity of a stroke is beyond comprehension. I still am in shock. Sometimes I long to do the blacktop or, better yet, go back to mowing the lawn and cutting the hedges.

Burnout Becomes Self-Defeating

My job was to push Herb harder and keep him from the dreaded plateau. This effort, and our own poor communication, increased an ongoing tension between us. The more I asked him to practice his exercises, the more he withdrew behind a passive mask. Sometimes he sat from one meal to another reading, watching TV, and making periodic grunts to use the urinal. My compassion and love wilted.

Herb's ever-present facial pain compounded my feelings of inadequacy and frustration. Too often when he halted his activities and sat at the table or on the chairlift, crying, I also broke into tears. *I cried often from loneliness, frustration, and fear. Pulling away from family and friends, I made fewer phone calls and felt little incentive to make it through the day. Sometimes I wondered if this empty shell of a husband and life as a martyr was all I would have in the future. At one point I thought about how easy it would be to let the car engine idle in our closed garage. We could sit in adjacent chairs in the kitchen, read the newspaper, and calmly wait for the carbon monoxide to spread. That would mark a fitting end to this punishment for both of us.*

At these low points, Herb repeatedly asked me to put him in a nursing home. That prospect grew more feasible as I worried about what would happen to him or both of us if I became ill or injured. After some research, I arranged a tour of a nearby assisted living facility, and together we met with the director. *It was sobering to visit the facility and recognize we were just a hair's breadth from making a commitment.*

Our psychologist saw I was fraying and discussed caregiver wear-out and illness.[36] She suggested I hire a permanent caregiver and get out more. *How? We were already paying many hundreds of dollars a month for at-home support and therapies. How could we afford more custodial care? Besides, what would I do with huge blocks of time? Lunch with friends was not enticing, and I was too exhausted to figure out what I most wanted to do.*

Later, as I considered the consequences of burnout, how it was eating at me and driving me to consider desperate acts, this extra expenditure seemed minor. In contrast, a care facility would cost many thousands of dollars each month.

I compromised and asked Otis to come three mornings each week so I could cut out by myself, take long drives, and wander through stores. Time away helped me to gain perspective, differentiate priority battles, and discard all the rest, *especially after I learned about Jacqui.*

Jacqui's Lesson

Just into the middle of our second poststroke year, Jacqui died. A sturdy woman in her mid-sixties, she was the caregiver for her husband. Jacqui had undiminished enthusiasm and was always positive, capable, and warm spirited.

We met the two of them at a monthly stroke club meeting, and I particularly enjoyed chatting with Jacqui about caregiver experiences. She became my role model. I admired her physical strength, psychological stamina, and indestructibility.

Jacqui walked out her front door one day to hang up an American flag. She suffered a fatal heart attack and lay outside by herself until a passing neighbor noticed. *I continually shudder for Jacqui and for all caregivers who die alone. After giving everything they have for another person, their isolation seems like the most awful injustice.*

---

[36] *"Time and Difficulty of Tasks Provided by Family Caregivers of Stroke Survivors," Journal of Neuroscience Nursing 36, no. 2 (2004): 95–106; http://www.medscape.com/viewarticle/474597_8*

A Caregiver's Lament

Rarely do spousal caregivers command much attention from others. We struggle through twenty-four-hour, seven-day marathon weeks, taming the aberrant into routine. To focus full time and energy on the stroke survivor, we often shelve personal needs and identity. Our silent fear is that, like Jacqui, we will die unattended and alone.

Friends and family ask, "Are you taking care of yourself?" In the early years, rather than complain about not having time for a quiet cup of coffee or to go to the bathroom, it was easier to change the subject.

Many people I've met do as I do: they struggle. Some employ full-time staff to dress and interact with their spouses. Others opt for nursing home custodial care. There are no "one size fits all" approaches. Financial circumstances, health, cognitive function, and age of both the survivor and the caregiver all affect the range of options. Psychological and financial burdens are great whatever the choice.

I chose to channel my energy, commitment, and intensity to push Herb to recover as many of his capabilities as possible. But enforced togetherness creates friction points we didn't have before and magnifies others already in place. As close as we had been in the past, we needed personal space and separate outlets. Now we follow one track, which for me has become slow and monotonous.

Frequent clashes threaten our relationship. For Herb, life is Hobbesian (nasty, brutish, and short) in stark contrast to his previous independence. My optimistic behavior rubs him the wrong way. He will scowl, grunt, reproach me in words, and glare as though I am the cause of his stroke. I have no patience for such behavior and petulance.

Discord between us has risen. I am often quite critical of her doing a certain task awkwardly. Then I remind myself, sometimes much later, that this was a chore I previously performed. Now, after forty-plus years, she's responsible. How could I be so insensitive? What does my defensive/aggressive attitude portend for our future relationship?

Seeking Professional Support

In one joint session, our psychologist asked Herb whether he was punishing me for his stroke. At first he blamed his anger on the clutter of notes I often leave on the kitchen counter and then on the clothing hangers clustered in the hallway waiting for me to bring down to the utility room. Later he admitted he vented his anger at me because he had no one else to blame.

Dr. Dreben asked Herb how many hours a day he thought I spent as his caregiver. Herb estimated ten hours. Then he launched into his familiar refrain that he belonged in a nursing home.

"With your noodle, do you think you would be comfortable in a custodial environment where you would hear people moan and groan through the long nights? Where the food is institutional and the support minimal? And where the monthly rates would be offensive to your sense of scale as an economist?" She suggested Herb owed me an apology.

We drove home in silence. No apology. Herb later napped and then insisted at the last minute we cancel our evening dinner plans with friends. I wanted to transform myself into the protagonist in the Tennessee Williams play *The Roman Spring of Mrs. Stone*. A new widow, she meets a young gigolo and flees from her life. Fortunately, Otis came for a few extra hours the next day so I could calm down and reflect.

Our psychologist repeatedly advises me to carve out more personal time and pursue my own interests. After three years the time has come, she stresses, to return autonomy to Herb for exercise, activities, and quality of life issues and go find new "home improvement projects." If he decides not to exercise regularly, then he has to live with the negative results. *Hey, that's risky. I've seen what happens when Herb exercises his prerogatives more than his body. He regresses!*

I often wonder if the situation were reversed how Herb would handle my stroke and dependency. Would he choose the same course I did and opt to care for me himself at home? I'd like to think so. No doubt, were he pushed he could figure out how to do household tasks, but the learning curve for medical and pharmaceutical complexities would drive him out of his mind. *Our psychologist is right. I often feel trapped. I have withdrawn from people and need to regain my intellectual and personal outlets. I used to chat with friends while cooking dinner. Now Herb sits at the kitchen table or naps in the living room and catches every word. It's not that I have secret information to impart, but his presence dampens a free exchange.*

Personal Fears

I worry about who will take care of me when I am ill. *It terrifies me to think that Herb is no longer my backup. We promised to go "two by two" into old age and die together. This imbalance wasn't supposed to happen. The idea is jarring that, like Jacqui, I may die alone waiting for a neighbor to find me.*

After Herb's stroke, I updated our respective living wills, durable medical powers of attorney, and legal power of attorney. I needed the latter just to talk with insurance companies and request copies of Herb's medical records. I also signed up for my own costly long-term care insurance to avoid placing double financial loads on our estate should both of us require custodial care at the same time (see Chapter 15, *The Costs No One Talks About*).

Herb's medical power of attorney was easy because I am the designee. Mine was not. I had to relegate my life-or-death decision to a family member who is geographically very far away. *More tears fell as I recognized how alone and vulnerable I am.*

Little Extra Self to Share

Our adult children lead their own lives, but there are times when they need help from a parent. And sometimes it would be nice to take care of our grandchildren for a weekend or even longer. I feel guilty for my constraints.

During my burnout shortly after Jacqui's death, Otis could see that I needed a rest and told me he would take care of Herb for a few days. I left on a blustery January morning and drove to Hagerstown, Maryland, an hour short of my northern Virginia destination. I checked into a motel, stretched out in a long, relaxing bath, and felt so comfortable watching television and reading that I skipped dinner. Peace and quiet were luxuries that I had dreamed about for almost two years.

The next morning I awoke refreshed, had breakfast, and resumed my journey. I visited our daughter Miriam, who was again pregnant and confined to bed rest. After two full days, I returned home and found that Herb and Otis had survived, and even flourished, during my first break.

Otis and I found it was surprisingly easy. The all-consuming task of taking care of me must be overwhelming, sometimes insufferable for Berenice, and it has to get to her. These breaks give us much-needed time away from each other. They are a needed break for her, and they're good for me, too.

The Reward of a Separate Vacation

On another occasion some months later, my brother and sister-in-law, sensing signs of distress, presented me with a deluxe, five-day trip to Aruba for two with only one proviso: that I not take Herb. Otis agreed to stay for the week, and I took Kathryn. We found snorkeling in the blue-green waters of the Caribbean very restorative. I even succumbed to the lure of massage and body wrap with many smiles and no complaints.

Our cardiologist recommended that I carve out at least two one-week trips a year by myself. *That suggestion now made more sense, and I ached to get away again.*

Six months later, as fatigue and depression again set in, I jumped at an all-inclusive spa vacation to Ixtapan de la Sal, just south of Mexico City. The one-week package included door-to-door pickup and delivery, probably its biggest selling point for me. I traveled alone and subsequently connected with a group of six wonderful women, all from the New York area, who had come together. Highly maintained on daily massages, facials, walks, yoga, aquatics, and stimulating company, I returned home refreshed and with plans to meet these new friends the following January.

Although Herb and I shared our past vacations, these more recent ones have taught me the critical importance of relaxing by getting away from the constant stress of caregiving.

Reinvigoration Works

I returned from Mexico committed to pushing Herb even harder toward independence. As a boost for us both, I insisted he dress himself in the morning and take on other personal responsibilities, namely, to use a urinal with one hand, by himself.

Berenice thinks it adds to my self-sufficency. I think of it as simply more hell and just another way to add to my misery. There are many of these tasks that are extremely burdensome, and my pain level always shoots up when I do them. What price must I pay for independence?

I now leave Herb alone for brief periods. Whether I choose to attend an exercise class, go to the library, or have dinner with a friend, I feel less restricted. Leaving two urinals and the cordless phone on a nearby stand, I unlock our side door and rarely travel more than fifteen minutes away. Herb has memorized my cell phone number, and I check in several times by phone.

Danger still lurks because he cannot handle an emergency on his own, but we've accepted this risk. Right now it is more important for both of us that we separate, particularly during times of tension, and this ability demonstrates growing autonomy for each of us.

Herb lacks the energy to do the things I want to do. Although we attend lectures and cultural programs together, I must develop new areas for personal stimulation. On most evenings when we are home, we have also begun to gravitate to our separate interests. Herb enjoys television, preferably basketball games, and his crossword puzzles. I prefer writing and reading.

Degrees of Separation

At a stroke club Christmas party only weeks after Jacqui's death, I saw her husband sitting at a table surrounded by friends. I expected him to be disheveled, unshaven, and unkempt. He looked well, was neatly dressed, and actively interacted with the people sitting around him. He was managing on his own and required only a minimal assist from his children. That, too, is part of the lesson: no one is indispensable.

Thank you, Jacqui. I'm a slow learner, but I am beginning to get the message. I no longer have to do everything for Herb. It is a disservice to both the caregiver and stroke survivor when we negate our own existence.

Lessons Learned

Caregiver time-out is mandatory.

Burnout is unaffordable for both you and your stroke survivor. Time off from a 24/7 working schedule is imperative. A caregiver must break away once in a while for longer periods of even a week or two to come up for air.

Choose your battles.

Personal grievances create unnecessary baggage. Differentiate big problems from small nuisances, and address only those problems that directly affect your stroke survivor's recovery.

Set priorities.

When caregivers get very busy and short of time, self-care comes last. Thoughtless eating and skipping meals, skimping on exercise, getting too little sleep, and failing to allow for some downtime can take the biggest toll of all on your immune system. Put yourself first because if you get sick, both you and your stroke survivor go down.

Share your feelings and find ways to vent your anger.

Sort through your feelings with a trusted friend, preferably another caregiver. You may feel guilty, thinking you should have recognized and done more to correct bad habits or symptoms that led to the stroke. You may also feel depressed and frightened of losing your loved one. It helps to talk out these emotions so they don't fester. Consider professional help if you are deeply depressed or feel frustrated confiding to friends not in a similar situation.

Ask for help.

Assume people don't know much about strokes, even willing friends. Share your needs, even when all you want is a hug, a few words of encouragement, or a drink with a friend. Accept help but be specific: a dog walked, a cup of coffee, respite care for a half hour. The window of opportunity closes after the first few months, and most people will stop asking.

Don't negate your own existence.

Serving as caregiver does not make you less of a person. As a human being you have value and needs in your own right. Although harried, pushed, and stressed, find whatever it is that helps you relax and recharge; specifically, create space for yourself, your personal care, meals, and pursuits you find relaxing. These can coincide with naptimes, but you may also choose to stretch your day by rising earlier or going to bed later than your spouse.

Cut as many corners as you possibly can.

Be realistic: you don't have to choose the hardest way each time. Other people will assume you can do it all, but you know you can't—and you don't want to. Concentrate on your stroke survivor, your immediate family members, and yourself, and feel free to reject other responsibilities.

Forget about guilt.

Guilt consumes more energy than caregiving and is a luxury you can't afford. You will make mistakes. We all do. Divide your world into life and death situations, and choose life. Don't sweat the rest.

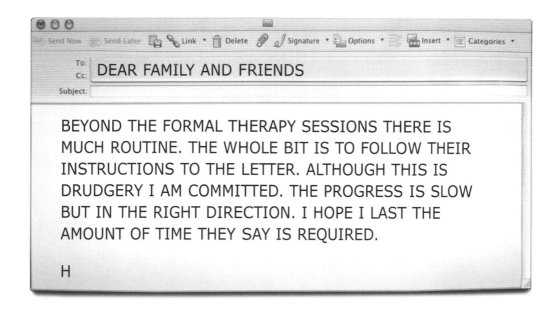

BEYOND THE FORMAL THERAPY SESSIONS THERE IS MUCH ROUTINE. THE WHOLE BIT IS TO FOLLOW THEIR INSTRUCTIONS TO THE LETTER. ALTHOUGH THIS IS DRUDGERY I AM COMMITTED. THE PROGRESS IS SLOW BUT IN THE RIGHT DIRECTION. I HOPE I LAST THE AMOUNT OF TIME THEY SAY IS REQUIRED.

H

CHAPTER 10
The Outpatient Therapy Program

Centimeter by Centimeter
We Inch Our Way Forward

Twice-a-week[37] outpatient rehabilitation at Metro lasted over a year and included all three therapies—physical, occupational, and speech—in consecutive one-hour sessions with a one-hour break for lunch and rest. We regularly met with Herb's rehab specialist for the first two years and continue to see his psychologist.

The occupational therapist moved Herb through a range of activities, including pulleys to strengthen his shoulders, arms, and hands. At the beginning he couldn't square his shoulders, but he worked hard and steadily improved.

I often sat at a center table in the big, open therapy room similar to the hospital facility but located in a nearby rehab facility for outpatients.

---

[37] *The twice-a-week sessions stretched sometimes into three times a week when the scheduler had difficulty fitting in Herb's consecutive appointments.*

Sometimes I participated. Other times, I read a newspaper or spoke with patients and family members who had sudden, life-changing encounters much like ours. People in this room represented a wide range of demographics and problems. Some learned to use new leg prostheses; others to recover deadened limbs from stroke and spinal issues; still others to coordinate and balance. Those who didn't exert themselves or who locked in at their level of capability quickly dropped from the program.

Under Medicare rules, the nasty word in rehab therapy is *plateau,* loosely defined by others who came before us as a failure to make progress. A physician must recommend and provide a written prescription to initiate therapy. The stated period often covers a dozen or more sessions. However, the program is renewable, assuming the patient advances within stated government guidelines. But should that patient simply lock in at any level, hence plateau, the therapy program stops.

Herb worked very hard to progress. He advanced from only a few limited steps to actually walking with his pyramid walker on one side and his therapist on the other. The practice street has a McDonald's fast-food mock-up along with real-world sidewalks, curbs, and alleyways. He also learned to walk up several flights of stairs. Descending was another matter as his therapist guided his feet on each step, first the left and then the right.[38]

Following Herb's left arm pain episode and subsequent angioplasty, he lacked energy and hit his wall. The rehab program discharged him with the helpful suggestion that he check back in six or eight months for reevaluation. Perhaps, they said, he might resume these therapies. We used the break to rebuild his strength and then moved to another program specializing in aqua therapy, which was much closer to our home.

Restoring a Mind

Kathy Grekco was Herb's speech therapist at MetroHealth's outpatient rehab center. Her program, which continued for many months after other therapies had ceased, was the most significant for his recovery. Before the stroke Herb thought himself a fine communicator, and afterward felt frustrated by his inability to exchange words and thoughts.

---

[38] *The therapy practice ascending and descending flights of stairs has proven vital in numerous power failures, when our chairlift does not work. We are well trained in both directions.*

As an early benchmark, Kathy taped Herb reading a short assignment, then played it back for a colleague unfamiliar with his voice. In six months, Herb advanced from a recognition level of under 40 percent to over 80 percent.[39]

At the beginning, as he was feeling humbled and useless, she and Herb discussed his career prior to the stroke. He instructed me to comb our office files for specific reprints of his many editorial columns and articles. Herb came into the next therapy meeting with an abashed smile and carrying a stack of opinion columns from various local and national publications.

From the start Kathy recognized Herb's capabilities and helped him reestablish the connections by building on his interests. Herb's cognitive functioning, although somewhat disjointed by illness, seemed otherwise intact. Rather than concentrate only on audible sounds, she tailored a therapy program specifically for him, focusing on language expression, word retrieval, organization, and sequenced thoughts. Her exercises guided Herb back to his word processor,[40] which offered him a faster, more direct means for organizing his thoughts and facilitating language expression than slurred speech.

At the beginning, he was reluctant to sit in front of the keyboard. It reminded him of the capabilities he felt he had lost. Shifting keys for uppercase text was impossible at first because it requires two well-coordinated fingers. Herb began with only one finger on his left hand and used limited punctuation. Tiring easily from effort and frustration, he worked his assignments for only brief periods but slowly persevered.

Sometimes as I watched him painstakingly working I thought about possible similarities between my husband and a retarded man in Daniel Keyes's novel Flowers for Algernon.[41] *Both Charly and a test mouse undergo a series of injections that helps them advance rapidly to brilliance. Their joint achievement rapidly regresses after the medication loses its effect. I agonized that, like Charly, Herb could also regress were he to suffer a second stroke—and I would lose him.*

---

[39] *Herb's speech, still guttural but now easily recognizable, has advanced to a 90 percent level of recognition both in person and on the telephone. He still has to work hard to form his sounds, and long conversations require lots of energy.*

[40] *Previously, Steve and Kathryn had each tried unsuccessfully to get Herb back to the word processor. Steve lugged his father's huge desk and computer up from the basement office, running cables to connect one level to the other. Kathryn and her husband, Chuck, after great research gifted Herb with a one-handed PC keyboard. Failing to master the complexities of moving from upper- to lowercase, he chose to stay with his two-handed keyboard.*

[41] *Called Charly in the 1960s film.*

In class and at home, my husband required assistance clarifying incongruities and redundancies in his responses. We saw a flash of the old Herb as Kathy slowly guided him through these exercises and the next, stressing cognitive flexibility and varied forms of written expression. Together they applied these lessons to business and personal correspondence. Later Kathy assigned tasks to enhance word retrieval and divergent thinking, and she required Herb to shift from general concepts to particular subjects.

Afterward she worked on sequencing events, logical thinking, and writing progression. Along the way, Herb became more facile with the keyboard and learned to punctuate as well as shift between upper- and lowercase.

Kathy is someone special. She began her lessons for me the same way my in-hospital speech therapist had. I expected a rerun of the exercises stressing pronunciation and sounds. Yet something about her was different. She went beyond teaching me to speak so others could understand me and helped me to find the cognitive road back. Kathy reawakened my thought process that for a length of time had remained dormant. Thank God for her.

Herb advanced to exercises that engaged his passion for theater. As one of his final tasks before concluding the speech program, and knowing that Herb is a fan of the playwright George Bernard Shaw, Kathy asked him to summarize one of the plays we planned to see at an upcoming Shaw Festival.

George Bernard Shaw was famous for the strong roles he wrote for strong-willed women....So, too, in Candida. She is the wife of the Reverend James Morell, who is the always pompous and all-knowing rector of a diocese in London about the turn of the century. He is continually doing good things, always of an uplifting nature. He is extremely self-complacent to the point of smugness. This certainty is carried over to his wife. Hers is the role of a proper wife circumscribed by his view of what is necessary to be always correct....

With increasing confidence, Herb submitted an article about an important computer landmark event to a local business newspaper, which the editor published as a bylined column.

...The IBM 650 was the new industry's initial thrust into the world of business, government, and educational applications. Computers were marketed as a tool for those with extremely large data-processing needs <u>and</u> the resources to pay the high asking price. Forecasters predicted that only a few organizations would require such a cumbersome mechanism, numbering in the hundreds and maybe even thousands....

Kathy distributed copies to physicians and therapists who had worked with Herb. As a massive stroke survivor Herb had far surpassed the expectations of others in this outpatient rehab program. She was among the first professionals who took a profound interest in Herb as a human being separate and apart from his physical limitations. With her help, he has come a very long way.

Aquatic Therapy Program

The Peter B. Lewis Aquatic and Therapy Center (PBL) is located only ten minutes from our home. Armed with a new Medicare-approved prescription, this time written by our internist, Herb attended therapy there twice a week for another year. He learned to do deep knee bends in the water on his weakened right leg. Therapists used an underwater treadmill to rebuild Herb's lower right leg and thigh muscles and assigned numerous home exercises. They underscored their point that contact therapy time is insufficient to reach desired goals without daily, at-home reinforcement.

Undressing Herb for his aquatics session and then showering him after the pool was a huge effort. During the colder months, he wore his bathing suit under sweatpants. I would whip off his outer clothing, including shoes and socks, and exchange them for water braces and sandals. Following the swim, and back in the unisex shower room, I would transfer Herb to the shower seat, then dry him off and dress him again. Once in, the shower took a half hour or so. Sometimes when two or more couples, husband and wife, or patient and attendant, waited before us in queue, our wait was much longer.

This wait was even more onerous than for medical appointments because I was wet and cold.

Overcoming the Plateau

After eight months, Herb no longer exerted a sustained effort and stopped progressing. In April 2003, Eran, his aqua therapist, discharged Herb, offering a conditional return, and stipulated that he would have to pull himself up out of the wheelchair to a standing position three times in succession. And by state regulation we would also require a new therapy recommendation from our physician. *Meaning more paperwork for me.*

We continued going to occupational and speech therapy appointments in an adjacent building, and we targeted a little ice cream parlor that stands at the opposite end of the complex, a walk of about 800 feet. I bribed Herb to walk the full distance with a prize of an ice cream cone. At first it took him almost one hour. Within only a few weeks, he reduced the time to just over twenty minutes. *There was a bigger issue here than his diabetes, and sugar cone or sugarless, the additional glucose was minor relative to this achievement.*

Once Herb was seated with his ice cream, I raced the walker back to the aquatics center and exchanged it for his wheelchair. Then I ran back and transferred him in time for his next appointment.

Within six weeks, Herb learned to push up from his chair, bending his head forward and lifting up from his hips and buttocks. He admitted great trepidation each time. He passed the test, we obtained a new prescription for Medicare, his therapist Eran performed a new evaluation, and sessions resumed.[42]

Occupational and Speech Therapies, Part 2

Herb's second occupational therapist worked for over a year to build strength in his hand, arms, and shoulders. Lisa wanted the increased strength to translate into greater personal independence. When she saw me place Herb's eyeglasses on his face and heard that I was still dressing him, she chided both of us.

---

[42] *Herb hasn't pushed up out of the wheelchair by himself since.*

She insisted that Herb learn to dress himself. Too often, she told me, the caregiver impedes progress by trying too hard, anticipating too much, and too eagerly responding to each request. Benign neglect became her order of the day. *Her advice was much the same as I had heard from Steve, Sara, various physicians, and almost every therapist who has worked with us. But how exactly was I to enforce this directive when his scowls, tears of frustration, and ratcheting facial pain drove me into steady retreat? Call me a coward, but I usually chose the easy way.*

I hated the dressing task from the beginning. It was very hard to get the sock on the right foot, particularly because I had no recourse with my right hand. It was hellish. It still is.

Lisa gave us two curved pieces of plastic; each had a rope and handle. My job was to fit each of Herb's socks over the corresponding form, arrange his other clothing, and walk away. The first time Herb dressed himself,[43] the task took over an hour and he finished drenched in perspiration. He subsequently reduced the task to ten minutes.

At Lisa's insistence, Herb was now regularly dressing himself. Although displeased with this abrupt change, he came to realize the benefits of his growing independence.

Lisa was good for me. She was sympathetic yet fairly forceful. She walked the tricky path of one who is both aware of my disabilities and yet can play the disciplinarian. I'm sure that I brought extra frustration to the task, but that's her job. She was indispensable, both for her official duties and particularly for her jovial nature. I'm grateful for her support.

Herb's speech therapist, Jaime, helped him increase his vocal volume and more comfortably hold discussions in person and on the telephone. His concluding assignment was to publicly ask a question at an upcoming continuing education course at a local university.

Speech has been a particularly difficult asset to lose. I always considered it as one of my fortes. Questions came easily. Now I find the effort to form and deliver a question in a public setting is huge, especially given my reduced stamina.

---

[43] *Dressing excluded heavy shoes that require two hands and a shoehorn.*

Prestroke, Herb was an active and thoughtful participant in such programs. We continued to attend after the stroke, and sometimes Herb whispered questions for me to raise. But he emboldened himself and prepared to tackle the microphone with his now slower and raspier speech. I overheard him practicing repeatedly. Sadly, a mechanical fault silenced the amplification system. Unable to shout his question, he postponed his reemergence for another year.[44]

Jaime, although I knew her for only a short time, was also a stalwart.

Occupational and speech therapies concluded just before our second year marker, and this time Herb graduated with honors. He had pushed himself to attain goals set by all three therapists. And he succeeded.

Postgraduate Exercise

We continued to take advantage of as much physical therapy as possible. We took a private membership at the aquatics center so that we could independently use their special fitness room. Our physical therapist prepared me as Herb's personal trainer with a program plan and special instructions on the varied Nautilus equipment. We are steady in our attendance and try to work out at least two times a week.

Sustained therapies keep Herb from being imprisoned in a nursing home. At the same time, he must exert great effort to maintain his current level and even more to advance. To do otherwise would mean regression.

New Opportunities and Next Steps

In January 2004, Herb became associated with a pilot program that is pioneering stroke rehabilitation research, a cooperative effort among the University of Maryland School of Medicine; National Institutes of Health; the Baltimore Veterans Affairs Geriatrics Research, Education and Clinical Center (GRECC); and the Claude D. Pepper Legacy Program. Also called the Claude D. Pepper Older Americans Independence Center, it is located in GRECC facilities, in downtown Baltimore.

---

[44] *We missed the following program because I was ill.*

Research focuses on a rehabilitation technique to "rewire" the brain and restore mobility by combining repetitive exercising of the paralyzed and nonparalyzed limbs together with rhythmic auditory cueing. This theory departs from more traditional therapy practice that emphasizes compensatory use of the functional limb along with the principle that rehabilitation is effective only within a few months following the stroke.

As a dramatically different departure, this program targets chronic hemiparetic participants (people who are paralyzed on one side) up to nine years after onset of their stroke. It uses special exercise machines and treadmills to move paralyzed arms and legs in a continuous and repetitive motion. Brain-imaging technology before and following participation measures whether the movement affects brain activity.

Program therapists in Baltimore trained us and allowed us to take the special device home to Cleveland. In turn, we promised to keep up the exercises three times a week and fax in weekly reports. Our initial six-week trial using the bilateral arm device stretched into four months because of bad winter driving conditions.

We have seen limited but encouraging results so far. Herb's ultrasound, in March 2004, only six weeks after starting the device, showed small but positive improvement in blood flow to both right and left frontal lobes. This test, one of many in a continuing series of ultrasounds to monitor his brain since the stroke, was the first to show improvement. We attribute his functional gain to the program. In addition, when Herb began to use the arm device, he could move his right hand forward a total of ten centimeters.[45] Within two months he had doubled his reach. In three months he extended it to twenty-eight centimeters.[46]

In May 2004, we returned to Baltimore for the second prong of this pilot program, training to apply repetitive motion to both legs by using a treadmill. Friends who had two treadmills gifted us with one. We adjusted the speed down to 0.3 mph and borrowed a special belt to hold Herb in place for the first weeks. Herb began at a one-minute walk although he had initially qualified by doing three minutes. By the end of the first week he

---

[45] *We tie his right hand around the control, using an Ace bandage to hold it in place.*
[46] *Otis and I discovered that we were each separately nudging up the control and forcing Herb to meet a continually moving target.*

lengthened his total time each session to five minutes; within six weeks he moved rapidly to fifteen minutes (in two sessions), and he continues to advance. He uses the treadmill three times a week with two spotters. Otis holds him on his strong left side; I stand behind, with both my legs on the rims and also holding the gait belt. Herb calls out the minutes and makes his own decision about how long to stay on. We fax in the reports monthly to GRECC and plan to return for reevaluation in six months.

I'm not crazy about this exercise. Berenice, along with Otis as co-conspirator, gets all excited by seeing the increasing numbers. They tend to forget that I'm not just a robot that they can program to go faster and faster. Yet progress is being made, so I continue.

Herb and I are especially grateful to Andrew P. Goldberg, MD, professor of medicine and director of the Claude D. Pepper Older Americans Independence Center; Richard Macko, MD, associate professor of neurology in the School of Medicine and director of the stroke program at the VA and the GRECC; and to Jill Whitall, PhD, associate professor of physical therapy and rehabilitation science, who led various aspects of the overall study. Their research, vision, inclusiveness, and flexibility demonstrate that strong, far-reaching recovery methods are under way for stroke survivors.

Assuming that Herb remains in a proactive mode, we feel confident he will continue to progress. We see improved results each week.

The exercises were tough but the people weren't. I definitely did not feel like just another "piece of meat" to be processed into a statistic by the system. Our caring and solicitous therapists share a highly personal touch.

Lessons Learned

Identify knowledgeable and caring therapists.

Search for therapists and programs willing to tap into the stroke survivor's interests as powerful motivation. Talk with them about reasonable goals and expectations and make sure you concur.

Supplement formal therapy programs.

Recovery requires tremendous reinforcement. Home practice must become part of the daily routine. Most therapists provide lots of homework. Use those materials to help you develop a daily program both during and after therapies conclude.

Get around the dreaded plateau.

Medicare and other insurance programs require that the stroke survivor make steady progress. Ask your therapist to explain these guidelines. As one program ends, find another with a different emphasis and request a new medical authorization.

Train your survivor to use a word processor.

Stroke survivors who have difficulty expressing their thoughts verbally may discover a communications outlet by using a word processor. Special keyboards designed for one-handed use may facilitate the activity. Some systems also utilize speech synthesis and recognition for those with little movement or voice.

Continue exercise after therapy programs conclude.

Don't slacken your efforts even after graduation from therapies. Find other programs and centers on your own and continue to progress.

Search for experimental programs.

The National Institutes of Health, Veterans Administration, and Claude D. Pepper programs are currently among a number now researching the effects of stroke and searching for methods to aid improvement. Ask your rehab physician, research the Internet and your library, and read stroke publications. These programs hold promise and do not limit poststroke achievements by timetable.

Learn when to step back and let your stroke survivor take over.

You can't and don't want to do everything. Gradually allow benign neglect to become the order of the day. Sometimes building independence is painful.

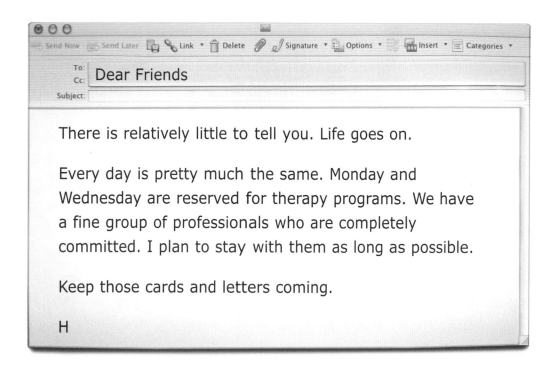

There is relatively little to tell you. Life goes on.

Every day is pretty much the same. Monday and Wednesday are reserved for therapy programs. We have a fine group of professionals who are completely committed. I plan to stay with them as long as possible.

Keep those cards and letters coming.

H

CHAPTER 11
Friends and Family

Finding Support When Your Back is Against the Wall

Stroke is a life-changing experience, and nothing is as it was before. Caregivers make choices because time and energy are so limited. Outsiders who contribute warmth and support are welcome; those who draw energy away are not.

Our family, friends, and neighbors continue to provide immeasurable support. Many have hovered about us from the beginning. Others disappeared after sending the token card or gift. Perhaps they worried Herb's stroke might be contagious. Or maybe they felt uncomfortable trying to hold a conversation with him.

I know I antagonized some people by not taking phone calls, but special, well-tested friends and family members continued despite my rebuffs. Discussions with immediate family took place by cell phone while I walked Dizzy early in the morning and late at night. Time restrictions likewise limited e-mail, but there at least with a few extra clicks one message could reach many.

Herb Responds

Eventually the time came for Herb to respond. *This breakthrough was huge! After all the efforts by Steve, Kathryn, and Herb's speech therapist to lure Herb back to the Internet, he finally succumbed and began to communicate on his own. Vocal and articulate, he needed this vital communications pathway.* The keyboard allowed him time to organize his thoughts and work out the message slowly and painstakingly. When he was finished, he asked me to direct it to people whom he chose from our address list. *Then I kissed him, threw my arms out wide, and yelled, "Yes, Yes, you did it!!"*

His first note, a one-liner without punctuation, drew a huge wave of responses. The immediacy of e-mail responses was a bit overwhelming but gave him great pleasure. As Herb regained strength, his messages lengthened. He learned to type with one finger, positioning the mouse on the left side of the keyboard and advancing from lowercase letters to caps and punctuation. I saw increasing evidence that his mind was functioning and he could still write.

This was an important step. Communication was an essential link between us and our relatives, friends, and professionals whom we picked up along the way. I <u>had</u> to find a means to reach others, not only to reassure them I was still alive but also functioning.

Problems Prompted by Home Visits

As friends and family began to visit, I studied their different reactions. Many lacked familiarity with stroke and seemed awkward and uncomfortable. Some spoke too much, as though compensating for Herb's slower, raspier, and often hard to understand speech; others filled in his sentences before he could; still others spoke too little in an effort to defer to his condition. It was difficult to prepare them for his psychological and physical changes.

Sometimes when several couples visited at the same time they conversed with one another and inadvertently shut Herb out of the mix. Later they whispered to me at the door that Herb seemed so quiet. Some asked if he was depressed. A few friends left similar messages on our answering machine, not realizing that Herb could turn on and listen to the machine by himself.

They were basically right: excluded from conversation, Herb became increasingly moody and impatient with these visits. With diminished vocal capacity, he felt he couldn't participate. He also found it difficult to follow staccato ideas when more than one person spoke at a time. As hostess, and preoccupied with serving, I was unable to guide the conversation. Left on his own, Herb retreated into a shell.

It was delicate. To participate in a conversation among several individuals, I needed first to make them want to include me. Even though the old Herbert is no more, I can still contribute if they make some small accommodation for me by giving me time to speak and then listening attentively. Carrying on a lengthy discussion under any circumstances is extremely tough. It upset me when others interrupted or carried on competing conversations as I was speaking.

I subsequently set ground rules. At the very beginning of a visit with both friends and family, I asked that they include Herb and allow him sufficient time to answer. To my amazement they often overlooked my request. I thought of reverting to a time-out whistle that teachers use on playgrounds. Instead, I chose to limit visits and gatherings to only two people at a time, often over small dinner parties.

Still, it was imperative that Herb master new skills and learn to stand up for himself. It took many months and much confidence building before he took the initiative to say, "Wait," or raise his hand to command attention.

Herb's psychologist suggested we invite people for dessert and tea rather than worry about all the attendant preparation for meals. Fewer distractions allowed me to more actively balance the conversation, though, in truth, sometimes I also forgot. But one glare from Herb set me straight. *It's so easy to get carried away. Caregivers are also starved for attention.*

This was a hard role for Berenice to follow because she always goes all out with guests. Now she had to limit herself to just dessert. It's an ongoing process.

We gradually began to venture from our home to meet friends at restaurants. I scout these out in advance for easy entrance, accessible restroom facilities, and low overall background noise. Friends' homes, on the other hand, are often the least accessible meeting areas. Most have steps leading to the front entrance, usually without railings. Some steps are too narrow; others are too deep. If there is a handrail, it is often positioned opposite Herb's good hand. Snow and ice compound the problem. Once inside, furniture arrangements often leave little room for a wheelchair or walker.

On several occasions, strong males carried Herb in his wheelchair up and down the front steps. More recently, after extensive physical therapy, Herb has begun to master a variety of front, garage, and patio steps on his own feet and with increasing confidence. We have learned to plant strong people in front, on the side, and behind him for added security.

New Friends

Through the stroke we have befriended physicians, therapists, and other stroke survivors. We met Mary Jo and Ken at a stroke club. Ken, a retired professor at an area university, suffered a stroke about a year prior to Herb's. Mary Jo and I engage in long telephone conversations and periodic lunches. We have an uncanny ability to discern when the other is depressed. Exchanging tales of our Sisyphean battles with the medical system lets off steam—more so than if we tried to explain these problems to "outsiders" who may give lip service but can't begin to understand the depth of our frustrations and challenges.

Neighborhood Comfort

The neighborhood sense of community reinforces our decision to remain in our home rather than move to a more accessible condo elsewhere. Neighbors have offered comfort and support in many different ways. A number have stepped forward to run errands, walk the dog, visit Herb, and share periodic dinners and desserts. During the blackout of August 2003, when most of the eastern United States and parts of Canada lost power and water, neighbors knocked on our door to check in and offer help. Some dropped off cases of bottled water. Others have told us to call them in an emergency, day or night.

In our former life, Herb and I often reached out to others in need. Now we are recipients. We try hard to express our appreciation.

We've happily hosted a dessert get-together for neighbors twice in the past two years. Herb is the host and enjoys addressing a few thoughtful comments to the group at large. People who have not seen Herb for many months measure for themselves how much he continues to improve.

Our friends, family, and neighbors have paved the way for Herb's reentry to the world with their patience, understanding, and thoughtfulness. In illness it is easy to wrap yourself up in a limited, wheelchair-circumscribed existence. It takes the good nature of others to tap on your door and encourage you to move out once again into the larger community.

People are concerned with their own lives. The onrush of attention at the beginning slowly shifts to indifference on the part of most. That's as it should be. The onus of living with this disability returns to us.

Lessons Learned

Don't isolate yourselves.

Friends and neighbors may feel awkward and not know exactly what to say or do, but they still want to visit. Arrange a short block of time for them to say hello. Don't worry about serving food. Also provide a departure signal, such as when you stand up, nod your head, or point to the door.

Establish ground rules.

People don't know what to say or do in the face of serious illness. Set up a few ground rules and explain them in advance. If the stroke survivor has difficulty speaking or following a conversation, suggest that only one person speak at a time, speak slowly, and allow time for response, whether it be in words, a grunt, or a head nod. Crowds are overwhelming and lead to discouragement.

Consider stroke clubs.

Seek new friends who share understanding and compassion with both caregiver and survivor. Many of the programs are informative and helpful. You'll meet people who understand your situation and can provide advice for particular needs and concerns.

Entertain over dessert and coffee.

Later in the recovery, as you feel more confident, arrange small gatherings under controlled circumstances. Make it casual and easy. Even consider disposable dishes. Empower your guests to bring the food if they insist.

Meet friends at restaurants.

Get around the hassles of difficult logistics by meeting in an accessible restaurant that you have scouted in advance. An outing offers a nice change of pace and avoids the awkwardness and fear of trying to handle inaccessible homes.

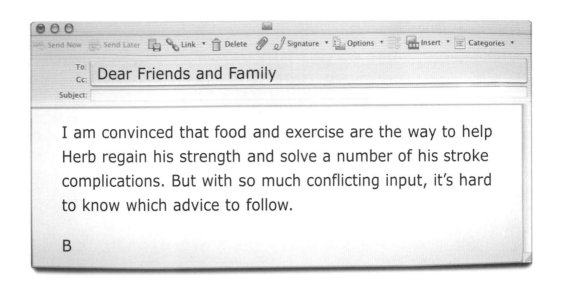

I am convinced that food and exercise are the way to help Herb regain his strength and solve a number of his stroke complications. But with so much conflicting input, it's hard to know which advice to follow.

B

CHAPTER 12
Food-Smart Recovery

If It Has No Salt, Fat, or Sugar,
It Probably Has No Taste...but So What?

A critical step toward Herb's recovery was learning to eat smart. Long-entrenched eating patterns simply had to change. Food intake affects the body's need for insulin and insulin's ability to lower blood sugar. Diabetes is bad enough, but discovering that high blood sugar can bring on another stroke caused me to draw a line in Herb's mashed potatoes and make diet a cornerstone of our recovery program.

To her a totally restricted diet, which also has no taste, is the way to go. Ugh!!

Long before the stroke physicians advised Herb to go easy on the meat, butter, potatoes, breads, sugars, and salt, with an overwhelming sense of invincibility, he chose to march to his own drumbeat. Herb used to travel on a comfortable expense account and entertain clients in costly restaurants around the world. Bread smeared with butter comprised his favorite appetizer everywhere.

Identifying Specific Needs

Following Herb's discharge from the inpatient rehab program, I went ballistic trying to follow all possible rules to bring down his high sugar and cholesterol levels. I bought many of the trendy books, including *Everyday Cooking with Dr. Dean Ornish* by Dean Ornish, MD, and *The Omega Diet* by Artemis P. Simopoulos, MD, and Jo Robinson. We also consulted with another Cleveland Clinic nutritionist who turned out to be a dietary zealot. She recommended a wide range of special foods that could not only lower bad LDL and build up good HDL, but might also reverse the thickening of Herb's arterial walls. The proposed diet consisted of low-fat, low-sugar, low-salt, and low-dairy products.

Taking copious notes, I organized recipes and ingredients, and then shopped at local health and organic food stores. From basmati and brown rice, Boca Burgers,[47] and wheat germ to bulgur, flaxseed, and soy protein flour, I bought everything on this new list. Then I cooked. Substitute muffins. Zucchini brownies. Baked fish. Broiled fish. Fish salad. I followed directions: small portions, frequent meals, limited protein, and no sugar.

I sought everyday choices in the reversal diets that offered alternatives to the traditional oil, sugar, and white flour combination that might still taste good. But I was surprised to find that low fat did not necessarily equate with low sugar. For example, one of the books listed a recipe for raisin-bran muffins that included multiple cups of brown sugar, molasses, and raisins. Any one of these ingredients exceeded our food constraints.

So began a continuing struggle—perhaps fight is a better word describing the tensions we have concerning food. Berenice became a zealot on the subject. Even small amounts of the wrong foods, eaten at widely dispersed times, are strictly a no-no. Entreaties to her that she is being draconian in her position are flippantly set aside. Anything that she feels will raise my sugar level, and particularly spike the reading, creates problems.

---

[47] *Meatless hamburgers.*

Discarding the Zealots

The next recipe book offered flax bran muffins (wheat bran combined with flax meal) and called for even more raisins and sugar. Obviously these recipe guidelines were not tailored to diabetics.[48] In desperation I combined both flax and wheat bran with low-fat yogurt, and added baking soda and powder. Instead of dried fruit, I substituted apples and cinnamon along with a sugar substitute. The heavy muffins tasted like sawdust. My experiment hadn't worked. However, the salvaged apple sections with cinnamon proved to be a winning dessert.

Our nutritionist stressed three key points: low fat because cholesterol blocks arteries, the cause of a possible next stroke; high fiber to lower cholesterol and also ease constipation; and low sugar to control Herb's diabetes. She recommended that all bread must be made with unrefined wheat. All crackers and pasta had to be whole-grain wheat. A portion of beef (permitted once per week) could be no larger than my fist. Baked potatoes must now be served bare and topped with sprinkled chives. She also advised me to include at least six to eight servings of vegetables and fruits per day.

Our dog, Dizzy, ate a wider variety of cooked vegetables than Herb, who believes that the world was created with iceberg lettuce, string beans, beets, carrots, and minimal spinach. All the rest are interlopers. Broccoli, Brussels sprouts, cauliflower, kale, collards, and cabbage, foods high in antioxidants, beta-carotene, and vitamin E, do not appear on his radar screen.

A periodic deviation from the prescribed "it's-all-good-for-you diet" wasn't asking too much. I just didn't believe that some divergence from the "so-called" good path was all bad, at least not if it was done sparingly and at great intervals. The battle lines were clearly drawn. She wanted only to serve me the all-good foods, while I wanted at least some respite from this thoroughly sugarless diet.

I searched to find appealing meat substitutes and still conform to guidelines espoused by both our nutritionist and these prominent authors. Two-bean enchiladas contain ingredients that Herb likes separately but repulsed him

---

[48] *Just a reminder that diabetics have a high incidence of stroke.*

when mixed together. Brown rice and shiitake pilaf never got to first base: the rice was the wrong color, and mushrooms were unacceptable. Even whole-wheat toast at breakfast was a failure. The worst reaction of all came when I served Boca Burgers on whole-wheat hamburger rolls. Herb's jaws clenched tight, and he said he preferred to go hungry.

The upshot was that Herb, an emaciated 143 pounds on his return home, again stopped eating. He had no appetite. Nor did I. The food I so painstakingly researched, shopped for, and prepared turned us both off. Meanwhile Herb's hematocrit[49] level dropped precipitously. Dr. Miriam Cohen, our Baltimore cardiologist, reported that Herb had critical iron-deficiency anemia. Several transfusions and thirteen iron injections followed. Subsequent bone marrow tests failed to indicate adequate reasons for this abrupt decline. With little definitive information, our internist attributed the cause to chronic illness and related complications.

I wondered whether the beef limitation might also be a culprit. Back again in the third year came limited amounts of lean red meat. Through Trader Joe's, a specialized food store that emphasizes high quality at competitive prices, we discovered buffalo burgers. Lower in cholesterol than beef, this entrée has readily passed Herb's taste test. His hematocrit level climbed six points within the next three months.

Pragmatic Solutions

After all my fruitless efforts to change our pattern of eating, I learned the most important lesson of all. One can win a victory but lose the war. Unless Herb enjoys his food, studies, preparations, and substitutions are useless.

Out went the books and the nutritionist. Back also came eggs, French toast, and pancakes made with egg whites—along with limited, low-calorie syrup. Lots of vegetables comprise our diet today, but we focus on the ones that Herb has always enjoyed: carrots, string beans, spinach, yams and potatoes. We use prodigious amounts of dried lentils, split peas, and lima beans.[50] Sometimes unfamiliar dark greens and root vegetables creep into his soups, but they are easily camouflaged by the food processor.

---

[49] *The hematocrit is the percentage of whole blood that is comprised of red blood cells. A low hematocrit can indicate various types of anemia, blood loss (hemorrhage), destruction of red blood cells, or malnutrition.*

[50] *I often substitute high-fiber edamame (soybeans), but Herb can't tell the difference.*

Our fare is rather Spartan since we stress lean meats and fatty fish, and substitute fresh fruit for baked desserts. But as I learn to use varied herbs and spices other than salt, the general taste is improving. We've eliminated most salt by substituting other seasonings. Although the saltshaker is not entirely abandoned, I use it sparingly. Today I read labels and use few prepared foods. We still enjoy exceptions, including chicken soup, which requires substantial table salt to bring it to taste, but we have it less frequently. Curry, cumin, turmeric, pepper, and lots of fresh garlic and onions are high on my list. Vegetarian soups now take precedence over those I previously made with beef and turkey bones. Sautéed onions in olive oil usually provide an ample substitute for the meat taste.

Herb misses his desserts. Two small pieces of dark chocolate compensate. Although he is not above begging, his doleful eyes don't exactly move me, but they do prompt other friends to periodically drop off freshly made cookies, trifle, scones, and even brownies made with Splenda sweetener. Assuming his glucose level permits, he can splurge once in a while. Then these gifts mysteriously disappear into the bottomless freezer to emerge on low blood sugar days. Sometimes they never reappear.

It's all a puzzle to me. I find that my traditional and lifelong passions in food are no longer desirable. Indeed, I must turn away from those labeled taboo, like ice cream, pies, and cake, altogether. Ah, these I would kill for!

The Good News

My reward comes in plotting Herb's glucose levels, which are now usually within normal ranges, albeit with oral medications. His quarterly hemoglobin A1c glucose rating remains at 6.0 and under, another significant measurement of our success.

But food controversies continue to confuse me. A recent public debate casts concerns on several popular types of fish high in omega-3 fatty acids: farm-raised salmon and canned tuna. The big question this debate raises is: does mercury poisoning offset the good omegas?

Perhaps the time has indeed come to limit our food intake to pure mountain water and chocolate, and abstain from everything else. But where can you find pure mountain water today?

Bean and barley soup is a winter staple and one of Herb's favorites.[51] Not terribly involved or difficult, it can be made vegetarian-style, as I prefer for our needs, or with meat.

Herb's Favorite Bean and Barley Soup
Vegetarian-Style[52]

2 cups dried lima beans	2 to 3 scallions
4 carrots	3 large fistfuls of barley
3 garlic cloves	Salt and pepper to taste
1 medium to large onion	1 tablespoon olive oil

Rinse lima beans carefully and soak in a large container of water overnight or microwave until softened (thirty minutes). Drain. Place in large pot, cover with water, and bring to boil. Cook on low heat for an hour, adding water and stirring when necessary to avoid sticking. Grate carrots, garlic, onion, and scallions by hand or in food processor using grating setting. Add to soup along with barley. Add salt and pepper. Pour olive oil in and stir. Bring soup to a simmer, gently stir, and forget about it for two hours. Refrigerate overnight so that spices blend well. Reheat; add some water for a thinner consistency, otherwise eat with a fork. Complement soup with slices of crusty bread. (If you are a diabetic, choose darker breads that have less sugar.) Carnivores can add a big soup bone at the beginning step.

Serves 6 to 8 and freezes well.

Good nutrition represents a major step in my husband's recovery. But I've learned through hard experience to mix common sense with the standard dos and don'ts associated with a well-balanced diet. It doesn't matter how nutritious the ingredients or the amount of preparation time. If the food doesn't appeal to your stroke survivor then your effort is wasted. *And yes, Herb, it is OK to bend the rules once in a while.*

In aggregate, good medical care, food, and exercise comprised only two-thirds of the recovery process. Quality of life issues came next.

---

[51] *I promised in our marriage contract that I would learn to make this Kleiman family favorite.*
[52] *Bean and barley soup is thick enough that even stroke survivors with swallowing problems should have no difficulty eating it.*

Lessons Learned[53]

Talk to a nutritionist about your stroke survivor's specific food requirements.

The more you know, the more in control you are. Before making any dietary changes, either seek help from a nutritionist familiar with your medical needs or independently research the foods and ingredients to avoid. Learn about portion size and how to limit certain foods while emphasizing others.

Always read food labels.

Bring a magnifying glass when you shop. Even foods that seem similar can have very different nutritional values, sugar content, and calories. Prepared foods, particularly the "low carbohydrate" kind, generally include surprise ingredients, such as sodium and fats, to make them tasty.

Choose worthy substitutes.

Diet is a key element in controlling blood sugar and high cholesterol. Low-fat dessert novelties made with sugar substitutes offer good taste when used in moderation. New buttery spreads from natural oils have no hydrated or trans fats. And ground buffalo offers a lean, tasty hamburger.

Seek foods that reduce high glucose and cholesterol levels.

Certain foods, such as dried beans, can actually bring down high glucose and cholesterol levels. Some fat is necessary for your diet, but choose "good" fat that is unsaturated. Just a little olive oil adds taste and eliminates "bad" cholesterol.

Don't forget the fiber.

Many highly processed foods have zero fiber, so necessary for regularity. Whole grains, fruits, beans, and other vegetables are high in fiber, which fights off bad cholesterol and minimizes chronic constipation.

---

[53] *Note: I am not a dietician, but as a caregiver I have learned certain dos and don'ts that work for us.*

Exercise common sense.

Common sense and compromise must coexist in modifying the stroke survivor's eating patterns and quality of life. Food should be appealing to eye and taste, whatever the dietary modifications. When food becomes boring or too regimented, it's just not worth eating.

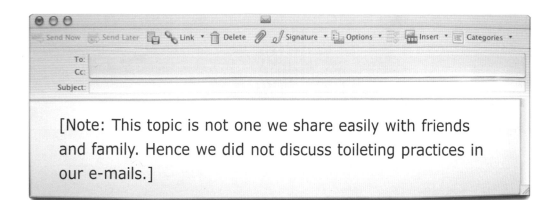

[Note: This topic is not one we share easily with friends and family. Hence we did not discuss toileting practices in our e-mails.]

CHAPTER 13
Toileting Nightmares

The World Is a Difficult Place, but a Little Help Wouldn't Be So Terrible

How I wish that somewhere in all the medical discussions, the literature, and conversations with other caregivers, someone had talked to me about the ultimate lesson in caregiver survival: Depends, Depends, Depends.

Urinary Frequency

Stroke attacks all bodily functions, but toileting is seldom discussed in lay terms. I learned much too far down our road to recovery, and after great anguish, that urinary frequency is a prevalent side effect. The toileting function became even more complex for us because Herb could not independently walk to the bathroom or, through much of the first two years, use a plastic urinal.

A significant portion of our lives still revolves around this now immortalized urinal. Five or six of these special bottles nest in prime locations around our home. Outside challenges in the first few years before I discovered Depend products were even more demanding. *Agonizing is a much better description.*

I thought I was going to go out of my mind with process and frequency. Like Lady Macbeth, I was always washing my hands.

Perhaps we are all born with toileting hang-ups. Nothing upset me more in the rankings of poststroke frustrations than impromptu toileting arrangements. No doubt my scowls and grumbling heightened Herb's own neurosis and anxiety. There was not a trip, visit, excursion, or walk where, right in the middle of things—and usually at the most inconvenient spot with the fewest hygienic conditions imaginable—he suddenly and absolutely had to go.

At first, the entire toileting experience seemed dangerous and frightening to me. With his poor balance, I worried that Herb might topple, striking his head against one of many sharp corners. Then, as we ventured from our home into the wider world, I found myself frustrated by the lack of available facilities to accommodate his needs.

Searching for Unisex Bathrooms

Because Herb has little use of his right side, poor balance, and only one usable hand, he requires assistance to walk, stand, sit, unzip, and wipe. While generally continent, Herb sometimes loses his ability to restrain himself. Urgency is a fact of life. At most, we have three minutes, and usually fewer, to find a bathroom, so speed is imperative.

Following inpatient rehab, Herb and I began a schedule of medical and therapy appointments. Even in large medical complexes, we were challenged to find handicap-accessible toilets that could accommodate both of us in the same room along with the wheelchair. Unisex facilities are not universal.

According to federal guidelines, a handicap-accessible bathroom must have both door and stall wide enough to accommodate a wheelchair. In real life these rules aren't enforced. Unisex/family/wheelchair-accessible toilets are difficult to find in the best of circumstances, and are often hidden at the end of long hallways and behind heavy doors. Most resemble broom closets. They often double as storage areas with boxes of toilet paper, hand wipes, and other cleaning paraphernalia piled to the ceiling. Hospitals and medical office buildings are the most flagrant offenders, but the problem is widespread.

Herb requires privacy and dignity in addition to speedy access. I require an easy means to empty and wash his urinal. Many buildings without unisex bathrooms lack larger handicap stalls that can accommodate a wheelchair. Too often I must wedge the front of Herb's wheelchair into a petite ladies' room stall and am unable to close the door behind us. My imperious "Give us just a minute, please!" holds off advancing troops but not easily.

Each change of environment imposes challenging problems. In Herb's first poststroke year, we decided to venture out to see the movie *Gosford Park*. Herb required multiple toilet runs toward the last half hour of the film. Friends thought I was joking when I asked how the movie ended. We tried again with *A Beautiful Mind*, but this time I read the book first, then accepted the interruptions. In each of the two theaters we found it easier to enter the women's room while the film was running rather than afterward, when the facility again filled with people.

Once I stopped at a local playhouse before a show to scout facilities. The house manager patiently explained that their men's and women's bathrooms were handicap-accessible and that an usher would be happy to accompany Herb. Not trying to be contrary, I clarified our need for a unisex bathroom. *Ye gods! I had to spell the whole need out in full detail leaving no subtlety as to why an usher could not take care of him in the men's room.* Resignedly, the manager unlocked a door and led me down a remote hallway. He assured me that the door would remain open for our later use and that a maintenance man would guide us through the inner sanctum.

During intermission, we found that the doors were locked. No amount of pounding aroused the maintenance man. Herb and I retreated to our car to use his plastic urinal in privacy. We drove away from that theater and didn't return.

Many of the restaurants and theaters we used to enjoy came off our list. Before the stroke, I thought nothing of running down a flight of steps in a restaurant to use the women's room. Now it becomes impossible to do with Herb.

Yes, we must compromise when unisex bathrooms are unavailable. But being thrust into a women's or men's restroom, even those that have handicap stalls, remains a continuing source of anxiety. During crowded times, women are none too happy to share facilities with a man. They silently stare; some twitter, children point, and know-it-alls explain that we've entered the wrong room. Still, women are generally more understanding than men, although more cautious.

Men's restrooms are unpleasant. Because open urinals are usually located close to the entrance, we must pass a crowd of exposed men, and they are not happy to see me walking through to reach the stalls behind. Sometimes we take the risk. If an empty men's room fills up, we'll hide in our stall until all other patrons have exited.

However, there are good places where handicap accessibility does work. The lesson I learned was to scout the facilities first, talk to managers, and seek their assistance in advance. The Blossom Music Festival, summer home of the Cleveland Orchestra, is one example of a responsive facility. Their operations manager drove out on his day off to show us around the grounds and demonstrate the complex's handicap accessibility and unisex bathrooms.

Toileting for me is an ongoing, complicated problem. Gaining access and privacy requires lots of coordination and cooperation.

Hazardous Stops While Driving

Urinary urgency has compelled us to stop on residential streets, turnpikes, college campuses, and in shopping centers. We have halted in the midst of stop-and-go traffic, rainstorms and snowstorms, and construction.

My husband doesn't usually say anything, but I watch his body slouch low as he grimaces and grunts. That's his silent shout. Once while driving on a freeway, we had just passed a rest area when he felt the need to stop. We pulled over to the side of the busy highway, always a dangerous option. He claims he cannot perform on demand.

Herb will generally carry the capped urinal between his knees. Even in a plastic bag casing, the urinal is not secure, and occasional spills have left a prominent odor in the car. *I don't begrudge the urinal, but I do resent a plastic bottle with a weak lid.*

Our most hazardous stop came in the middle of a terrible snowstorm while returning from therapies at MetroHealth. The trip started under clear conditions and was preceded by a bathroom stop. Expecting we would drive home without further demand, I'd carelessly tossed my backpack on the backseat, far beyond immediate reach.

We encountered gridlock only a block or two after our highway exit. In the midst of this blizzard, with no obvious pull-off available, I caught sight of Herb grimacing, grunting, and slouching. How was I to grab the backpack from the backseat, retrieve the urinal, and hold it in place while we inched forward? When I finally put the car in park for a few moments, our stop prompted a cacophony of honking horns. Back in the safety of our garage, I put my head down on the steering wheel, relieved that we had made it home safely, full urinal and all.

Creative Dryness

I spent months devising a way to keep Herb dry for several hours at a time when toilets and urinals weren't available. The urologist prescribed a variety of medications from Detrol LA to Flomax to lessen the urinary frequency, but due to side effects we have discontinued both.

Our psychologist urges Herb to relieve himself in advance of a car trip, restaurant, or other excursion. He insists he cannot. I figured there must be mechanical devices for more effective control along with the medications. Surely others experienced similar needs before us.

We went back to the urologist, who suggested a range of penile attachments resembling instruments of medieval torture. Each condomlike apparatus required exacting fit. I was advised to wrap a tape measure around my husband's penis to determine total inches and corresponding size. Each style attached differently. Some had a button; others utilized sticky tape. The bottom of the condom connected to tubing that, in turn, emptied into a plastic bag. The unit attached around the thigh and waist.

None worked well. These devices are designed for immobile patients, and they disconnected with minimal movement, creating a gush of urine. Herb was devastated. *I was none too happy cleaning him up from top to bottom and later disinfecting the car.* In winter, the cold made these mishaps even worse.

All were instruments of terror conceived at the height of the Inquisition. I tried them and they were too awkward to use. I was mortified that a simple bodily function had transformed itself into time-consuming embarrassment and self-doubt. How would other, more complicated chores and functions work out? I felt devastated.

On our own we tried Depend, the adult diaper. To provide extra absorption I inserted a feminine super-super napkin. Decades ago, this procedure helped our then-toddlers sleep comfortably through the night. I subsequently discovered that Depend makes an insert specifically tailored to adults. The combination works well, but the downside is a perceptible ammonia odor when activated. A built-in deodorant would make a welcome addition.

Initially, I worried that use of adult protection would make Herb feel even less a responsible adult than before. However, recent articles about incontinence among professional men and women have helped lessen the stigma. While the products are not perfect, we've finally gained some measure of time and security.

Depend has brought the outside world much closer and removed many prior restraints. *And it has helped me to feel less stressed out!* We can now sit through an entire movie or play, take drives in the country, and even participate in a lecture without panicking about when, where, or how quickly we must find relief.

The solution was unwieldy, self-deflating, and awkward to put on—but it worked. I still cannot get used to the thought of my wearing diapers, just like a baby. I guess I never will.

The Second Half of the Equation

Bowel movements conjure great sensitivity on all sides, and the world is even less forgiving. While Steve was home he tried to help his father become more toilet independent, insisting that Herb learn to wipe himself. To our son, powerlessness meant abrogating this very personal function to another person.

Bathrooms are not easily conducive to Herb's needs. I believe that he has to accommodate to the situation wherever possible, and he has. However, Herb has infrequent irritable bowel syndrome that again raises the issue of urgency. It would be much easier to stay home and not confront toileting challenges on the outside, but that's self-defeating. We choose to confront these obstacles. With time, I've learned to regulate Herb's diet, carry extra wipes and toilet seat covers in my backpack, and strive for a toileting pattern. As Herb's self-control improves, these situations become less frequent. But the outside world remains a daunting challenge.

Becoming an Advocate

Sometimes fighting is justified. After being locked out of handicap-accessible bathrooms during an evening performance at the Cleveland Museum of Art, I called the executive director and talked with her assistant. The museum's security head contacted us, asking how the museum might better address our needs. Herb and I carefully thought through several areas where the museum could improve, and we then made a proposal.

At our suggestion, the museum invited us to speak before a special training/ sensitivity program for security guards. Herb and I discussed our situation and the problems we've had locating an accessible bathroom and finding a responsive guard.

We also mentioned several other difficulties, including entering and exiting the museum's heavy front doors. *I remain bewildered by the indifference of many people who stand around and don't offer to help. It takes so little to hold a door open for a wheelchair or someone on an unsteady walker. A similar indifference (or lack of foresight) characterizes the design of many buildings that cater to the elderly and disabled. We constantly encounter doors in medical complexes, theaters, museums, banks, and restaurants that are heavy and hard to open. Try pushing a wheelchair, bracing a walker, or holding a gait belt while grabbing one side of a door to keep it from closing on you. Even more treacherous are automatic doors timed to normal pace, which close even while you are slowly making your way across the threshold.*

The guards, at first surprised to hear from us, became a receptive, thoughtful audience. Their subsequent questions ranged from particulars about accessibility problems on the main floor and elevators to the ease of viewing text from the wheelchair.

Herb and I are gratified that on our return visits security guards rush to open doors for us and other disabled visitors. Handicap-accessible bathrooms now remain open, well lit, and marked by appropriate signage all day and throughout evening performances.

With time and patience we are overcoming obstacles one by one and rediscovering our old world. As we proceed we also try to make it a little easier for others with similar needs who follow.

Lessons Learned

Depends, Depends, Depends.

Adult protection is a fact of life. With it you can travel, attend exhibitions and performances, and not worry about "accidents." Don't leave home without it. Look for the ones with side tabs for easy application and removal even while the person is fully dressed.

More reasons for a backpack.

Choose one with multiple zippered compartments. Carry a urinal, wipes, plastic gloves, and toilet seat covers along with a change of clothing, if necessary. The bag attaches easily to the back of a wheelchair.

Scout facilities in advance.

We now work harder to anticipate our needs. Don't assume that restaurants, theaters, and museums address your needs automatically. Call ahead; visit the facilities; make your needs known.

Become an advocate.

Public indifference often stems from a lack of familiarity with specific needs of the disabled. Should you encounter situations in public areas that are not handicap accessible, complain to the proper authorities and ask what corrections they plan to make.

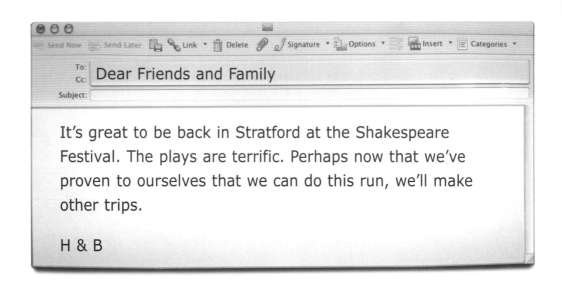

It's great to be back in Stratford at the Shakespeare Festival. The plays are terrific. Perhaps now that we've proven to ourselves that we can do this run, we'll make other trips.

H & B

CHAPTER 14
Travels with Herb

Discovering a Widening World

Before his stroke, Herb and I loved to travel, explore historic sites, enjoy great theater, and see the world. Even when we had little money, we were easily satisfied at a small inn with a shared bathroom down the hall. Travel became easier and more luxurious as our income increased, but we remained thrifty and in our middle years often piggybacked vacations with business trips.

Today international travel has moved beyond our reach. Long stretches sitting on airplanes threaten blood clots; narrow aisles are dangerous for a pyramid walker; and airplane toilets simply do not accommodate our needs. *Besides, with Herb's medical problems we want to stay within easy reach of our specialists.*

Even short hops don't seem worth the cost or the effort, especially when factoring in additional time for early arrivals, security checks, and transfers to a rental car while transporting wheelchair, walker, and suitcases. *I suppose we could do an air trip if we really tried, but it seems like a tremendous push. The little golf carts can't accommodate Herb, and I really don't want to work that hard pushing a wheelchair down the long walkways.*

It seems faster, easier, and generally more convenient just to drive. No longer spur-of-the-moment people, we plan our trips far ahead, particularly to secure handicap-accessible hotel accommodations. Family homes are generally off limits for overnight stays, given their steps, narrow bathrooms, and tight bedroom arrangements.

Hotels have become my nemeses. Rooms for the handicapped must address a wide range of special needs. Seldom do we find wheelchair and toilet/ shower accessibility. *I sometimes think that a blind veteran who smokes like a fiend represents the disabled prototype for hotels.* We've also crossed many leading hotel chains off our list because of staff indifference. Too often we have scheduled arrangements through a toll-free central number and later discovered they had not passed along our handicap request. Although I expected stronger support through the Americans with Disabilities Act (ADA), I've come to realize its limitations.

Our specifications include a nonsmoking[54] room, early check-in, portable high-rise commode fitted on top of the toilet seat, toilet bars, and roll-in shower. Even if assigned the correct room, which is rare, we must wait for a maintenance man to carry in and position the toilet seat extender and requisite attachments. Sometimes it still bears stains from the previous user. On other occasions we'll wait while yet another member of the housekeeping staff carries in a separate chair for the roll-in shower. As another hassle, we require extra towels, especially to dry the bathroom floor after a shower and before Herb stands up. Our order is not passed along to housekeeping, and we must make a new request daily.

Particularly at the beginning, this process was a learning experience. We learned to contact a top manager with a specific set of requests. We would secure his agreement but that didn't guarantee anything. The hotels simply do not cater to these exceptional needs.

---

[54] *We've found few handicap-accessible rooms that are also smoke free.*

Painful Experiences

Our most painful experience took place at a wedding of the son of close friends. We followed all the steps. Our specifications were agreed to in advance, and at check-in I confirmed the list before providing my credit card.

The registration clerk at this upscale hotel chain assigned us a room on the eleventh floor. I questioned why a handicap-accessible room would be on one of their highest levels, in case of fire when elevators are shut off. He assured me that the hotel monitored the locations of special needs guests and in an emergency would send people to evacuate us.

The first room had neither roll-in shower nor commode. The bellhop called down and requested a second room. Another floor, another long walk to the far end of the corridor.[55] The second room couldn't even fit a wheelchair through the front door.

Muttering that he was missing tips, the bellhop again called the desk. We went through the process four times before we found a suitable room. I was exhausted. I remember commenting to Herb as I checked out the bathroom that the floor tile had a shiny glaze and looked slippery even when dry. I called it an accident waiting to happen.

The next day, toweling Herb's legs following his shower, I crouched on the wet floor that I'd tried to dry with the few towels allotted to us. Suddenly my legs shot out from under me, I fell back, and my head, shoulder, and back struck the hard tile floor just missing the sink. I lay immobile, trying to figure out how badly I was hurt and asking God, *"Aren't I doing enough? What more do you want?"* The fall was hard and I was afraid to move.

A Tailspin When the Caregiver Gets Hurt

Injury is one thing. Injury to a caregiver is another. As I lay on the floor, I tried to think about how to get help. Herb couldn't move. He couldn't pick me up or yell for help. The front door was bolted. Neither of us could reach a phone. Could I possibly crawl to the phone and then raise myself up to unbolt the door?

---

[55] *Why do hotels regularly position handicap rooms at the end of corridors?*

When I finally opened my eyes, Herb was terribly upset. Although in shock, I felt no pain. The next day soreness set in, making the four-hour drive back to Cleveland hell. Not only was I the driver, but also the person lifting the heavy wheelchair into and out of the car trunk and making all the other preparations before and after the trip.

The physician at our local urgent care center reported that I had gigantic hematomas on my back and buttocks, but no sprains or fractures. He said I looked as if I'd been struck by a car going forty miles an hour. His prescription was to use ice and take over-the-counter pain relievers as necessary.

While I was examined and x-rayed, Herb waited by himself for almost two hours in the outside reception room. Vulnerable and alone, he was enveloped by self-pity. He worried about what to do if he had to use a toilet. When I emerged, I found him white as a sheet. *Instead of recognizing his fear, I interpreted his anger as impatience. I thought of the countless hours that I spent waiting for his appointments. Only later did I begin to realize how abandonment might feel from his perspective.*

I endured weeks of pain as we continued Herb's therapies and our regular routine.

Another Attempt at Advocacy

It took a letter to the CEO of the hotel corporation to generate response beyond the standard form letter from their claims department. The executive office referred my correspondence down the line to the hotel's general manager, who had been on vacation during our stay. His apology was the first and only one I received, and I told him that if the hotel modified their handicap-accessible room we would not sue.

The manager claimed that a corporate design committee familiar with ADA requirements approved both the tile and the location. But he agreed. *I simply had no time or energy to bring a negligence suit against the hotel. My first priority was taking care of my husband. Any other effort would be an unnecessary and costly distraction. But, yes, I lusted to get even for the pain and suffering that continue to haunt me.*

This was an example of hotel bureaucracy at its worst. From check-in to our accident incident, the hotel was concerned only with its efficiency—or the mock resemblance thereof. The most exasperating aspect was our going from room to room to room, trying to find the right one, even though Berenice had called them in advance with all the details.

Moving On

With research and good luck we have found kinder, gentler accommodations in cities we visit often. Hotels generally do not charge more for handicap-assessable rooms, but on occasion we will willingly pay a little more than standard rate to get a larger room with a separate sitting alcove. That allows me to indulge my late-night reading habit without disturbing Herb.

Most of our longer trips are pointed east to the Baltimore–Washington, DC, corridor for family visits that we piggyback with medical and therapy follow-ups. Whether we grow even more venturesome by car and surpass our self-imposed eight-hour maximum remains an open issue. Prompt access to specialized medical care presents a key consideration. While I hope never to redo our ninety-mile-an-hour race back to the Cleveland Clinic, that frantic run remains indelibly inscribed in my memory.

With the proverbial one-tank gas trip, we seek wheelchair-conducive vacations that center on theater, concerts, and university lectures. *It's great to be back behind the wheel, and it's relaxing for both of us. But, as with everything else in our lives, I'm learning to draw limits and not stretch beyond what I find is easy and comfortable.*

People are generally oblivious to the handicapped. I know I was before the stroke.

Lessons Learned

Make motel/hotel arrangements directly through in-house reservations.

The local hotel is usually more responsive to handicap requests than a central toll-free office that guarantees only a room and does not have specific room information to meet your needs. When you call, ask to speak with the in-house desk supervisor or manager. State your requirements (i.e., handicap-accessible, nonsmoking room with high-rise toilet seat and bars, roll-in shower, shower seat, and refrigerator[56]), and specify if you want guaranteed early or late arrival. Request a formal acknowledgment by fax, e-mail, or letter confirming these details. It will come in handy on your arrival should you find certain arrangements lacking.

Exercise caution in accepting floor assignments.

If your stroke survivor is wheelchair bound or on a walker, consider what might happen in the unlikely event of fire or other catastrophe, when elevators are shut off and stairs offer the only accessible means of escape.

Request extra towels.

Towels keep the bathroom floor dry after a shower, especially when the floor lacks a central drain. Ask for double the number you require, and hide extras in a dresser drawer. You won't have to wage the same fight daily.

Keep a travel file.

Keep a record of hotels with specific room numbers that have met your needs. This information will come in handy when you or someone you know makes a repeat visit. Request the room number directly through in-house registration.

---

[56] A small room refrigerator is particularly useful if you have medication that must be chilled and/or you require special foods.

Discuss special food restrictions with the restaurant chef.

If you have special dietary limitations and plan to take most of your meals at the same hotel or restaurant, it is helpful to work through dinner choices with the chef, preferably in advance.

Recognize your travel limitations.

Travel, whether by air or car, requires planning and arrangements, packing and unpacking, and lots of solo responsibility. Recognize your financial and energy limitations and seek ways to ease the process.

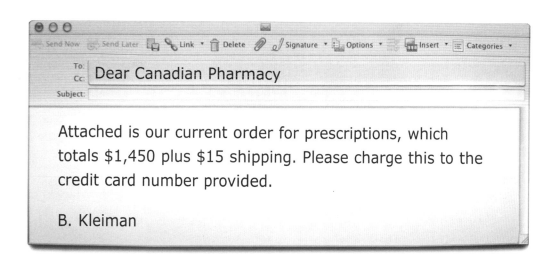

To: **Dear Canadian Pharmacy**
Cc:
Subject:

Attached is our current order for prescriptions, which totals $1,450 plus $15 shipping. Please charge this to the credit card number provided.

B. Kleiman

CHAPTER 15
The Costs No One Talks About
Plan Ahead

We expected our golden years to be fruitful, productive, and challenging. Retirement was not in our plans. And we gloried in finally reaching the top level in Abraham Maslow's hierarchy of values—self-fulfillment.[57] Herb and I intended to operate our strategic marketing business until, we joked, "we go out with our boots on."

The World Turned Upside Down

With the stroke came myriad responsibilities tumbling onto my shoulders. During the initial months when Herb was oblivious to the broader world, I couldn't ask him where he filed certain information or, when I did locate a file, how to process it. Fortunately, I had knowledgeable professionals to turn to, specifically, our broker and accountant, who provided vital counsel.

---

[57] *Abraham Maslow is known for establishing the theory of a hierarchy of needs, writing that humans are motivated by unsatisfied needs, and that certain lower needs must be met before higher needs. According to Maslow, general types of "deficiency needs" (physiological, safety, love, and esteem) have to be satisfied before a person can act unselfishly. Once you attain these basic rungs, you can then climb toward self-actualization. Note: I reference Herb Kleiman's thesis written in fulfillment of his MBA degree.*

Herb's timing was lucky: at the onset of his stroke he was almost sixty-seven and already on Medicare. Had we remained on our previous health care insurance and *not* had an excellent supplemental policy, our savings would have evaporated.

For the first few months, when Steve and Berenice took care of me at home, I worried little about the financial tasks. I had no feel for all the details Berenice was concerned with, nor did I care.

Emergency funds cushioned the first two months. My biggest financial concern was which funds to draw upon for home adaptations. Withdrawals from retirement accounts or random sales of securities carried significant tax implications.

Business clients questioned whether we might resume work when things settled. That hope grew increasingly unrealistic. My energies were focused on Herb, and I had no time to tackle projects other than those already promised. There would be no further earned income.

I learned to use Quicken software, a valuable tool for categorizing and logging checks, credit card receipts, and out-of-pocket cash expenses related to Herb's health care and home-adaptation needs. Organized and tabulated, these expenses comprise a substantial IRS deduction. Out-of-pocket expenses accumulated quickly, especially hospital parking fees, meals, and incidentals.

Because of earlier financial decisions, Medicare and our supplemental AARP policy would cover most of Herb's major medical costs, assuming he did not exceed the allocated number of hospital days. Although forced into retirement, we had sufficient funds to live comfortably.

Lifesavers: Medicare and AARP Health Care Supplement

I've heard complaints over the years about Medicare Part A and Part B program limitations.[58] Personally, I am deeply grateful to the United States government for an amazing safety net during cataclysmic illness. Medicare

---

[58] *Medicare Part A covers inpatient hospital care, home health care, and hospice care; Part B covers outpatient medical facilities, office visits, and related tests. After the annual deductible, each negotiated rate requires coinsurance of 20 percent.*

covered Herb's hospital and rehab expenses in full, along with costly specialists, medical tests, surgeries, home health care, durable medical equipment, and extensive therapies. Medicare and the American Association of Retired Persons (AARP) have to this date not rationed care or declined even one legitimate expense.

Before Herb reached his sixty-fifth birthday and after considerable research, we selected AARP's "J" program as our Medicare supplement. The most expensive of AARP's options available in Ohio, the plan supplements the remaining 20 percent for all medical A and B bills approved but not fully paid by Medicare.[59] AARP also negotiates pharmaceutical caps and, after the $250 deductible per person, pays one-half the cost of pharmaceuticals up to a maximum of $3,000. This negotiated rate alone provides significant cost savings.

A number of our friends opted for supplemental insurances carrying no monthly cost. Several companies withdrew from the market in the late 1990s, forcing subscribers to scramble for new coverage and pay a higher monthly rate than had they initially signed up with AARP on their sixty-fifth birthdays.

Medicare changes enacted by Congress in 2004 are confusing and may yet go through various gyrations as the full cost for prescription coverage under privately administered programs is completely tabulated. There is ample precedent for caution.

Herb's monthly fee for Medicare and AARP insurances currently totals almost $400, excluding deductibles. Although substantial for us on a fixed income, it is considerably less than our former insurance program under our business umbrella, and the benefits are better. In contrast to many less expensive health care programs, we have flexibility to choose specialists and consultants in other health care systems and states.

Pharmaceuticals, a Huge Drain

Herb required twenty medications daily with an average cost of almost $1,500 per month for the first two poststroke years. With prenegotiated

---

[59] *Medicare accepts, rejects, and negotiates lower rates for procedures, then pays 80 percent of the negotiated rate. AARP pays the remainder.*

AARP prices, it seemed to make little difference where we filled our prescriptions. For convenience I chose a local pharmacy. The downside was that Herb quickly exceeded his plan's $3,000 reimbursement maximum within the first six months of each year. We were on our own, albeit at an agreed-upon rate, for the remaining period. The time came to seek cost-saving initiatives and stretch his maximum to cover as much of the year as possible.

Step 1: *Split Pills*

Our internist suggested that I purchase and halve double dose tablets for greater value since many drugs cost the same regardless of dosage. A $5 pill splitter easily cuts most tablets.

Step 2: *Consider Canadian Pharmacies*

With mostly nongeneric "designer" pharmaceuticals on Herb's list, my next step was to purchase prescriptions directly from Canada. After researching articles, online price comparisons, and personal recommendations, I chose Mediplan Health Consulting (RxNorth) as our supplier. The Canadian pharmacy maintains our faxed prescription lists, ordered in quarterly refill quantities. I call their toll-free phone number (1-888-773-2698), fax in new prescriptions, and charge the bundled reorder to my credit card. New prescriptions generally require three weeks, and renewals take two weeks or less. AARP reimburses one-half the cost of the three-month supply minus the delivery charge.[60] The savings are sometimes as high as 50 percent per order over local and chain pharmacies. Canadian prescription costs have increased with the decline in value of the U.S. dollar and as pharmaceutical manufacturers attempt to limit Canadian exports. Costs of medications in our local pharmacies are rising even faster.

Step 3: *Ask Your Physician about Lower-Price Alternatives*

We ask our physicians whether generics might substitute for more expensive and well-advertised brand-name medications. Generics are often less expensive here in the United States, particularly at some national chains and local discount pharmacies, which accept AARP's negotiated prices. One large warehouse chain, Costco, lists pharmaceutical prices on the Internet for ease of comparison.

---

[60] *I send a cover letter to AARP with the amount for each of our orders and enclose copies of Mediplan's receipts. AARP reimburses us directly.*

Step 4: *Buy in Bulk*

You can find discounts when you purchase in bulk. Check the pricing and find the cost of each prescription by dividing number of pills into the total cost. Use this comparison analysis when evaluating possible benefits. But use this purchasing method only for standard pills that you feel confident you will use. Test a new drug by starting with the smallest possible quantity.

Step 5: *Request Samples*

Pharmaceutical companies provide many samples to physicians. When starting on a new medication, we test it first in smaller quantity for adverse reactions rather than discard a three-month supply. In addition, I request samples of current prescriptions at the end of each appointment. Sometimes samples can cover as many as three or four additional weeks in savings. Over the course of a year, these savings have sometimes added up to $1,000.

Step 6: *Prune the Pharmaceutical List*

We've had specialists whom we rarely see again prescribe medications. These prescriptions can easily continue into perpetuity. At each visit, we ask our internist and cardiologist to review our list of medications and recommend which, if any, we can remove.

Step 7: *Maintain Contacts with Local Pharmacies*

Pharmaceuticals that have been on the market for a long time, such as Herb's long-acting nitroglycerin capsules, are often priced so low that large chains and Canadian pharmacies find little incentive to carry them. Local pharmacies oblige us with convenience, fast fulfillment, and accessibility. We turn to them when there isn't a huge price differential or with new prescriptions that must be filled immediately.

Step 8: *Contribute Unused or Unfinished Prescriptions*

Organizations in your area (such as free clinics) can benefit from prescriptions that you've abandoned before their expiration dates. Your contribution may be a tax deduction.

Step 9: *Investigate Patient Assistance Programs*

Various drug companies offer special programs, called patient assistance programs (PAP), that discount certain pharmaceuticals. Criteria vary with each company. Type the company name into Google or another search engine to find a direct link to the appropriate home page. (For more general information on PAPs, go to www.rxassist.org or www.needymeds.com.)

Medical Bills Require Careful Examination

Quicken accounting software greatly facilitates record keeping and allows a convenient method to monitor previous payments. I log each check, credit card receipt, and out-of-pocket expenditure and then track how much we've paid, the dates, to whom, and for what purpose. I turn over my cash flow report along with a detailed list of pharmaceutical and health care expenses to our accountant at the end of the year. The total of medical and dental expenses substantially reduces both state and federal taxes.

I also store Medicare and AARP statements chronologically by most recent first. This system also allows me to track repetitious or erroneous statements. I was raised in the old school that invoices must be paid promptly. But I am frequently aghast at health care billing procedures. Invoices shoot out quickly. Credit for erroneous bills inadvertently paid by a patient is issued tardily, if at all.

Health care institutions prepare and mail invoices long before insurance resolutions provide closure. These bills are often riddled with errors. Some problems eventually sort themselves out. Others you have to fight to resolve because they involve hundreds and sometimes thousands of dollars. I've also appealed Medicare rulings on behalf of several health care institutions when I thought they were shortchanged. In one case Medicare denied a hospital claim of almost $6,000 because of a technicality.

If the patient is fully covered both by Medicare and a supplemental plan, there should be little or no reason for your health care provider to invoice you. But it takes time and energy to protest. When we receive statements I believe are in error, I generally do nothing for a few months. If statements repeat monthly, I eventually call and insist upon speaking with either a supervisor or the head of the billing department. Customer affairs representatives are generally unwilling to check past records and follow up with insurance providers. Their bosses take on this responsibility. If they don't, the next step is to refer the problem to the hospital's financial ombudsperson or chief executive officer.

One hospital turned our account over to the bill collector although I made repeated efforts to clarify the errors with the head of billing, the financial ombudsperson, and even the specialist. Upon receipt of the collector's first "official" warning, I called and requested an itemized statement of arrears. We've heard nothing since.

Final Thoughts

When Herb and I planned for retirement, we did our best to project our future financial needs. In some respects, we were far off the mark. For example, more than half of current expenditures never appeared on that list of future costs. Also absent was the long-term care policy that I initiated for myself just prior to my sixty-fifth birthday. We simply assumed our good health and business would continue indefinitely. We didn't factor in the cost of chronic and debilitating illness. Had the financial maven reviewing our projections suggested we include an additional $40,000 per year for all the ongoing health care expenses we now face, I would have scoffed.

Today, unplanned expenses cut into discretionary funds. We find ourselves caught in a medical vortex and can only hope these massive expenditures ease with time.

I am grateful, however, that we had the foresight, means, and discipline to save for retirement and lock away a substantial rainy-day retirement cushion. Current operating costs are relatively modest compared to a nursing home that might well run $8,000 monthly.

I continually tell Berenice to spend whatever is required. We worked and saved, particularly after we formed our own consulting company, and prepared to enjoy our golden years without incurring financial burdens. Admittedly, I did not anticipate the severity and depth of our current needs, but we're still solvent.

Lessons Learned

Plan ahead.

Save as much as possible with the knowledge that rainy days do come. Long before illness strikes, choose your health and long-term insurance policies wisely. Make sure your finances, will, durable medical powers of attorney, and insurance policies are in order with appropriate forms signed and notarized. Both spouses must know the amount of savings to draw upon and how to locate pertinent records and files, e.g., all bank accounts; mutual fund, and brokerage holdings; safe-deposit box; vehicle titles; home mortgage; medical insurance; life insurance; Social Security benefits; retirement and annuity benefits; credit cards and travelers checks; unpaid salary, IRAs, 401(k), pension, and profit-sharing; workers' compensation benefits; and will. Discuss plans with your family lawyer, financial adviser, and accountant in advance.

Keep multiple copies of your durable medical power of attorney[61] and living will on record.

Stroke gives little warning, and you don't want to find yourself searching for lost records in the midst of your shock and loss. Make sure critical information is clear and accessible to both partners before a medical catastrophe. Copies should be on file with your internist, hospital of choice, and in your home records within easy reach. Keep one copy in the medical records loose-leaf binder.

Establish a formal power of attorney document.

This legal authority permits the operating spouse to sign legal documents, request medical information, and handle other formal transactions.

---

[61] *Rules vary from state to state. Make sure your durable medical power of attorney complies with your special state regulations.*

Keep accurate tax records.

Use accounting software and maintain accurate, updated records. Hire an accountant well versed in health care expenses and deductions.

Comparison shop for your pharmaceuticals.

Check all prices carefully and consider the steps toward cost savings that you'll find listed in this chapter. At the very least, use a pill splitter and order tablets in double dosage.

Discuss pharmaceutical needs with your physicians.

Enlist their support to prescribe quarterly prescriptions that you can purchase in bulk. Bulk purchase usually saves money, but, before you order, check for adverse side effects and whether you will require that prescription for the full period.

Use generics whenever possible.

Physicians often prescribe the newest and most expensive medications when a generic will do the same job. Question both your physician and pharmacist about workable substitutes.

Invest in long-term care insurance for the caregiving spouse.

Whatever the other expenses, this one is basic and concerns your own future needs.

Monitor medical bills vigilantly.

Know your insurance coverage well and take time to assess whether incoming bills are legitimate. Mistakes happen.

Don't pay rogue medical bills.

You are entitled to an itemized statement, even a daily one, if necessary. If the billing department does not correct bills that you can prove are in error, contact the hospital's financial ombudsperson. Request the representative's name and a written record of the correction. Keep track of each person to whom you've spoken. Use a full sheet of paper and list date, name, and related comments.

Disregard mounting financial statements and pressures while your bill is in dispute. As a last resort, write or call the chief executive of the medical facility that is giving you grief. Many companies now have specialized customer-service SWAT teams that field comments directed to that office. Rest assured that your complaint is not their only one.

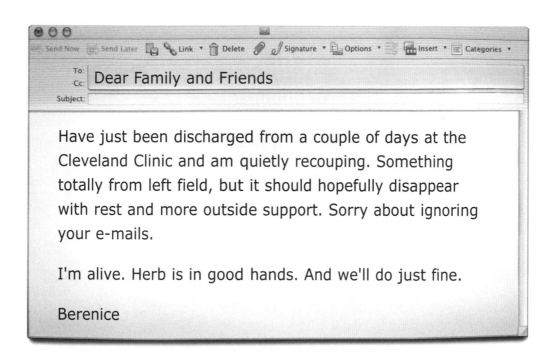

Dear Family and Friends

Have just been discharged from a couple of days at the Cleveland Clinic and am quietly recouping. Something totally from left field, but it should hopefully disappear with rest and more outside support. Sorry about ignoring your e-mails.

I'm alive. Herb is in good hands. And we'll do just fine.

Berenice

CHAPTER 16
What Happens When the Caregiver Gets Sick

When the Bough Breaks, the Cradle Will Fall

Early on a Sunday morning in our thirty-second poststroke month, I was awakened by a strange leg cramp. I roused myself and tried to walk it off, but, as the day progressed, pain advanced down my leg, making it increasingly difficult to stand.

I managed with Herb's chairlift and pyramid walker to carry up breakfast and lunch for him and let the dog out for his breaks. But by dinnertime I couldn't lift my leg.

That afternoon I had tried unsuccessfully to call Otis to ask for his help. I became more frantic. Our closest neighbors were out of town. I felt isolated. Herb needed urinal container changes and was beginning to grump at me because he hadn't eaten dinner. I tried to think about whom else to call but hesitated because a snowstorm was creating whiteout conditions.

I felt hugely impotent. Prestroke I would have been at her side doing whatever was necessary. Berenice apparently was too overstressed from taking care of me to take time out for herself. I would have given her time, energy, or whatever assistance was needed to help tide her over. But here I was, helpless to provide support in her ailment and still needing others' assistance. I worried selfishly about "What happens to me if she gets really sick?"

Calling for Help

Around 7:00 p.m. I finally reached Otis. Even with poor road conditions, he came immediately. First he helped me pivot my way to the bathroom and back. Then he took Herb downstairs for dinner. During that interval, I lay with one leg up and the other on the floor as I considered my options. The pain seemed much like what I had experienced from thrombophlebitis in the same leg some forty years earlier.

Finally at 11:00 p.m., with Otis's promise to remain with Herb for however long was required, I dialed 911. I remember requesting that the emergency medical service not sound their siren or come accompanied by the fire truck because I didn't want them to disturb our neighborhood. The team arrived within only minutes. I grabbed my cell phone as they carried me out on a gurney.

That night in the hospital I dreamed that Herb and I were in adjoining rooms in a nursing home, both of us in wheelchairs. I remember yelling, "Hell no!!" The sound of my own voice awakened me. I realized, as I lay helpless and alone in the big hospital, that there was no one but me to notify our children. What if I were to be seriously ill or die?

No one knew where I was, and Herb could not do much to contact them. *Other than Otis, I had no backup. I never expected that I would be the one lying in the hospital bed. Gripped by fear and with heart pounding, I thought about what a crappy way this was to die. Then I thought again about my friend Jacqui.*

Dodging a Bullet

After three days the specialists formed an uncomfortable consensus. They said I had septic arthritis[63] and required immediate hip surgery. Since I had had an anti-inflammatory injection and could now move my leg, I refused surgery. As a caregiver, I chose to return home and agreed to certain provisos. I promised to take anti-inflammatory medication, immediately return to the emergency room at the first sign of pain or fever, and see a hip joint orthopedist within three to five days following discharge.

Herb and Otis picked me up later in the day, and we went home. On our way, and at my request, Otis stopped at the local pharmacy, where I limped out to fill my prescription. In this day of photo credit cards, here was one more job I had to do for myself.

Otis stayed for the next two nights and then returned daily for the next full week. Fortunately, with lots of prepared food in the freezer, he and Herb managed quite well. I took life fairly easily with no lifting, lots of rest and reading, and unbelievable amounts of sleep.

Neighbors and friends chastised me for not calling them when I needed help. Surrounded by flowers and their thoughtfulness, the realization deeply warmed me that we had wonderful Otis and amazing people around us whom I could call on day or night in an emergency.

But just to be extra sure, I scheduled a home interview with a nursing service and began the process to become a client. *Suddenly facing my own mortality was terrifying. I realized that I was not as indestructible as I'd believed, and that my poor health or injury could easily destroy our fragile balance. Were I unable to care for us, we would have no other recourse than for both of us to go to an assisted living or nursing facility. The entire experience shook me profoundly.*

---

[63] *Septic arthritis is a potentially fatal infection of the joints characterized by pain, fever, chills, inflammation and swelling, and loss of function in those joints. It is considered a medical emergency because of the damage it causes to bone as well as cartilage, and its potential for creating septic shock.*

Fewer than three months later, even though I had adhered strictly to the specialists' ground rules, I suffered a second episode. This time I had emergency phone numbers and a ready plan. Fortunately, I was discharged quickly. *But I am still frightened and remain cautious. I take medication to prevent another occurrence, but should it happen, I am ready. I have my physician's pager number, emergency medication, and a backup plan. Herb's application is on file with an assisted living facility in case I am hospitalized a third time and Otis is unavailable to take care of him. The thought is chilling. Meanwhile, I push Herb toward greater self-reliance for his sake and mine.*[64]

Watching my indestructible wife in pain made me realize that life without Berenice would be no life. There are so many aspects of her care and support that I've taken for granted before and especially since the stroke. Even when I'm at my most depressed state, her confidence buoys my spirits. Without her, I wouldn't try.

Lessons Learned

Be aware that caregivers also get sick.

Caregivers are not the indestructible, invulnerable people we think we are. Bad things can and do happen. Keep an active, updated file of pertinent information in case you are incapacitated and someone must step in. Include a list of your care responsibilities and daily medications, organized by time of day, the name of your stroke survivor's primary care physician, and copies of corresponding insurance cards arranged in a small three-ring notebook. Place this information in a prominent place familiar to your stroke survivor and respite care worker.

Choose the people to contact immediately if you become ill.

Keep a list of telephone numbers for family members, close friends, and physicians whom you can contact day or night for help. Make the list easily reachable in case of an emergency—in your wallet, on your night table, and

---

[64] *Within the same year, I had another seven episodes and four emergency runs, each involving a different part of a limb and each meriting a different diagnosis, from trocanteric and palindromic bursitis to gout and beyond. Fortunately, although these episodes were very painful, they usually responded to an anti-inflammatory pill.*

on the speed dial of your cell phone. Be sure these people have a house key in case you cannot open the door yourself. Also let several neighbors know where you hide your emergency key.

Develop an emergency support plan.

Personal emergencies are unscheduled and can upset the best of intentions. Work out your plan on paper with directions, medications, schedule, appointments, and key people to be notified if you are ill. Add this plan to your medical binder as a guide when you are away. Discuss the plan with people on your list.

Plan for the worst.

Make long-term care plans for your stroke survivor as if you were to become seriously ill or even die. Choose a care facility and file the necessary forms so that you've established a record in case you are unable to do so later. However, because these facilities operate on a space-available basis, be aware that they may not have a vacancy during your emergency.

Prepare and freeze extra meals to cover several days. Also maintain several extra days of medications in your pill container.

To:
Cc: **Dear Dad,**

Subject:

Have met someone special. He's a good guy, and I know you'll like him once you get to know him. But it may take you awhile because he has a bit of a temper. So please be patient. I'm bringing him home next weekend.

Love,

Berenice

[An imagined e-mail[65]]

CHAPTER 17
One Stroke, Two Survivors

Men and Women Were Created to Go through Life Two by Two

Sometimes I am asked why I've fought so hard to reclaim Herb's mind and spirit. That is an easy question to answer. I have loved Herb since the first day I met him, even though he was then, and still is, irascible, hardheaded, and stubborn. From the beginning Herb and I formed a combustible team. Friends euphemistically referred to both of us as "strong-willed." That hasn't changed. He can erupt instantaneously, but my fuse takes longer. When I get upset, I do so with greater intensity and for longer periods. What brought us together despite our hardheadedness was an insatiable intellectual curiosity, a similar framework of values, and mutual attraction.

---

[65] *Had e-mail capability been available in February 1963, this is probably the note I would have sent to my father.*

◄ *Herb graduated in 1957 from The Cooper Union where he earned a B.S. degree in electrical engineering.*

▶ *Berenice sat for a formal engagement photo in February 1963 following a three-month courtship.*

◄ *Berenice and Herb rushing off to begin their honeymoon, June 30, 1963.*

◀ *Berenice became selective about her chocolates early in life.*

▲

Herb, as a teenager, didn't think much about either chocolate or girls.

◀ *Herb and Berenice pose with rehabilitation psychologist Dr. Elizabeth Dreben (center) and speech therapist Kathy Grekco (right).*

(Photo courtesy of Kathy Grekco)

Herb and Sara share a typical laugh. ▶

Herb works his New York Times crossword puzzle in ink.

(Photo courtesy of Marc Golub)

Steve, who came as soon he received my call, remained to help us through the difficult initial months.

Our grandsons. Zachary and Max, Miriam's children, play in a field of buttercups.

Kathryn and our grandchildren, Jonathan and Rebecca.

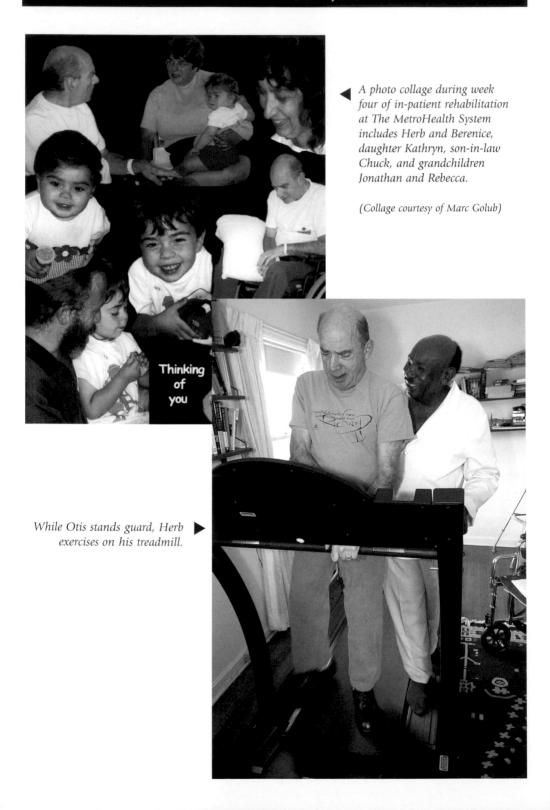

◀ *A photo collage during week four of in-patient rehabilitation at The MetroHealth System includes Herb and Berenice, daughter Kathryn, son-in-law Chuck, and grandchildren Jonathan and Rebecca.*

(Collage courtesy of Marc Golub)

While Otis stands guard, Herb exercises on his treadmill. ▶

Ours was a traditional and a passionate relationship. We saw in each other someone who was both physically and intellectually attractive. Berenice was perfect for me: smart and curious, liberal in her thinking, diverse in her interests, and, remarkably, her tastes were quite similar to mine. So within three months we were engaged and married in another four.

Mutual trust and challenge have long formed the wellspring from which we draw our strength. Had Herb and I not shared such an intense relationship, I doubt whether we separately and together would have the emotional ferocity to claw our way to poststroke survival.

We are blessed with a long marriage, successful business careers, three wonderful adult children, and four amazing grandchildren. Our two-person consulting business paved the way for us to live our dream of independence, stimulation, and financial reward. In our naïveté we fully expected to continue along the merry road, enriching the rest of our lives with work, grandparenting, and travel.

Starting with few resources, Berenice and I achieved financial independence and our relative self-sufficiency through the 1987 establishment of Kleiman Associates. We thrived as equal partners of a marketing–public relations firm serving high-tech companies in northeast Ohio and nationwide.

We relished controlling our own destinies. From a home office, where clients came to discuss business and often stayed to socialize over lunch, we enjoyed our work and built satisfying professional relationships. We felt we were finally approaching Maslow's fifth level of satisfaction, doing what we <u>wanted</u> to do.

Herb insisted that even with a heavy and profitable workload we allocate time for vacations. We traveled internationally every other year, sometimes exploring new areas and at other times catching up with old friends in Japan, England, Ireland, and Israel. We also visited our children and other friends, and enjoyed annual theater trips to the Stratford and Shaw festivals, in Ontario.

Between us, we hold three advanced degrees and lots of intellectual curiosity. To keep our minds sharp, we regularly took college courses locally and sometimes chose university alumni programs as vacation destinations. On more than one occasion, Herb devised a plan for us to separately enter and sit on opposite sides of the classroom. During discussion we debated one another. It was great fun to let off competitive steam in a controlled environment.

It was strange to be a student when I was usually older than the professor. From my earliest years teachers were special: they imparted knowledge. As I grew older they became somewhat less esteemed but still in a privileged position. Most important, we acquired knowledge for enrichment, not because it was another rung on the ladder to success. We vowed to never stop taking these courses.

We served as active participants in our community. Each of us assumed leadership of professional and not-for-profit organizations and guest lectured at area universities in subjects encompassing our professional and academic pursuits. We also wrote frequent op-ed columns for local publications. *Herb wrote many more than I did, which fostered more than a little goading and gloating on his part.* Separately, I wrote plays and greatly enjoyed a fully staged, professional reading for my first play at an area theater. *Enjoyed? I was blown out of my mind!*

Herb's massive stroke abruptly ended a comfortable transitioning to our so-called golden years. With his catastrophic illness our lives turned upside down and inside out.

Getting Back on Track

Herb's behavior for the first two-plus years can best be described as passive. He initiated nothing, noticed little, and although he joked with others who came into our home, he avoided any discussion with me. His behavior struck me as terribly unfair since I, too, suffer from his stroke. He has lost his independence, freedom of movement, ability to drive a car, and everything that made him feel like a functioning, vital man. But in addition to collecting a boatload of responsibilities, I have lost my best friend, my husband, and my lover.

Toward the end of the first poststroke year, with our anniversary approaching, Herb was more depressed than usual. He said little. But after one of Sara's visits, the day of our thirty-ninth anniversary, he perked up. Returning from therapies, I found a large vase filled with magnificent long-stemmed "American Beauty" roses and wrapped with a huge red bow at the side door. Red is my favorite color. A big broad smile lit Herb's face. He and Sara had pulled off the surprise of the year! I *cried. After so much heartache and so much incredibly hard work, Herb showed he understood and wanted to reach out to me. And he accomplished this surprise even without access to his credit card or wallet.*

Several months later, I discovered a beautiful birthday letter waiting at the office printer, located in our basement. Although I have cherished every letter and note Herb has ever written me, this one was different. The letter marked the first time he acknowledged both his situation and mine. The letter was beautifully composed. *As striking and meaningful as his underlying thoughts were, Herb's message demonstrated that he could once again communicate his thoughts brilliantly. This huge breakthrough must have taken him many attempts to complete.*

Life changed much for you, too, on July 14, 2001. It was abrupt and drastic, about as sharp as you could handle without losing your own sanity....Let's face it, I'll never be the same again. Probably I'll never drive again; I will never walk again normally, and my right hand most likely will never write again. These changes came so rapidly that we couldn't anticipate their severity.

...But you have responded with loving kindness and taken it upon yourself to be my continuing caretaker. Another woman might have committed me to an institution, albeit a good one....You chose to take on the much more difficult task of caring for me completely, a sometimes thankless task....All the minutiae of life came down crashing on your head. I watch as you tend to these chores, and I wonder how you do them. Your willingness to take on the tasks amazes me.

On the rare occasion that your frustration comes through, usually I have contributed to the matter....

Life will never again be the same as it was before the stroke, but Herb's flowers and letter gave me hope that we might yet carve out a new relationship. Our combustible tempers still spawn many arguments, especially over my demands that he push himself more physically rather than passively watching television. *I don't see my husband as less of a man than he was before. He may be physically limited, but his mind functions well, and I refuse to allow him to succumb to self-pity. The going is tough for both of us.*

Reclaiming an Intimate Relationship

We have separately and together found great difficulty navigating this very sensitive area. There is little in the literature to help us.

Sexual relationships were never discussed as a major subject (nor even a minor one) during my entire stay at the hospital or rehabilitation center. The topic was not talked about by any of my doctors, nurses, therapists, or other staff with the exception of Dr. Dreben, with whom I had some open and quite candid conversations.

Given Herb's obvious and not-so-obvious limitations, even with the best of motivations, how could we resume an active intimate relationship? *And did we want to?*

We came from an age where sexual discussion was restricted to the bedroom (for married couples), and it didn't go past there. The lack of poststroke medical discussion left me terribly ill-prepared for the most persistent question of my convalescence: could Berenice and I resume a sexual relationship?

With the stroke I entered a wholly new and strange world. For my entire seven-week in-hospital stay and the first two to three months at home, I was totally indifferent to any changes in my routine. I was preoccupied with just living and performing the very simple tasks and downplayed any other consideration, especially sex.

At first I was preoccupied about the simple lack of physical function. Needless to say, I had suffered severe physical losses that restricted me, especially in my ability to roll over with ease.

More than anything else, I worried about Berenice's reaction. Would she consider me less of a man now?

Our rehab psychologist encouraged us to share our thoughts and fears and suggested innovative ways to surmount physical limitations. Even more of an obstacle is an imbalance of timing and interest. Herb, who takes afternoon naps, goes to sleep much earlier than I and awakes in the morning much later, has lots of energy. I crave books to lull me to sleep. *It is odd to have to admit that some of the biggest hang-ups are mine. Fatigue is a huge one. After a long day as a caregiver, I often just want crawl into a nonfunctioning cocoon at night.*

It is hard to switch off caregiver reactions and romanticize over the same person I watch suffer in pain and agonize in depression. *Quite candidly, it is incredibly difficult to step beyond the caregiver baggage where I am responsible for Herb's needs, including toileting and personal care. Where is the line between service and love?*

Gradually we've talked through our mutual needs. With time we've discovered that at this stage of our lives we both strive to reclaim intimacy and our special connection to each other. It feels reassuring and wonderful to once again bed down, sharing the warmth of our bodies. Perhaps more will come as recovery becomes easier.

Lessons Learned

Understand the link between depression and loss of sexual interest.

Both the caregiver and the stroke survivor can lose interest in activities that they once shared, including sex. Decreased energy, fatigue, and burnout are symptoms of both depression and exhaustion.

Seek outside professional support.

Look to your rehab psychologist or internist for insights and support as you wrestle with sexual doubts and perhaps even a fraying personal relationship. Supportive counsel allows you to air frustrations and clarify hidden thoughts.

Value the stroke survivor's needs.

It is critically important to talk through and share your differing perspectives. Even with few words and limited action, search for those areas that can restore intimacy, warmth, and perspective.

Resume slowly and mutually.

Both of you need to feel comfortable and willing to reach out to each other. Whatever the physical limitations, you can find ways to share warmth and love.

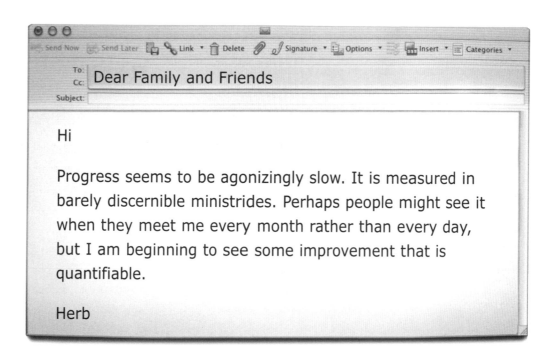

Hi

Progress seems to be agonizingly slow. It is measured in barely discernible ministrides. Perhaps people might see it when they meet me every month rather than every day, but I am beginning to see some improvement that is quantifiable.

Herb

CHAPTER 18
Restoring Self-Reliance

As Long as an Inchworm Moves Forward, It Progresses

Prior to his massive stroke Herb lived a vital, intellectually challenging life and felt in control of his destiny. But overnight, and seemingly without obvious pain or discomfort, his personhood evaporated. He found himself trapped in an unresponsive body without sufficient voice to beg even a bedpan. The stroke stripped away everything that in his view made him a man. This huge loss of ability to walk, talk, drive a car, care for his most basic needs—even to make love—rocked him to his basic core.

With prospects for a worthwhile life now bleak and hopeless, he despaired and debated whether to go on living. Two years later, still wrestling with his dependence and slow progress, he reflected:

Why didn't I just die? Things would be very difficult for my wife for perhaps a year or two, but ultimately she would be free to carry on. My progress is slow—very slow. A cadre of professionals has provided the services needed to at least help me help myself in the most basic of tasks: dressing, walking, eating, bathing, and much more. They can take me so far and then I level off. Even these limited, small steps are achieved with much effort by the therapist and only hesitantly followed by me. The easy retreat to a totally dependent state is ever present, providing a way out of the tedium of always pushing, always fighting to reach a status that is a fraction of "normalcy." This option continually beckons.

The Value of Setting Goals

From the beginning our son, Steve, and I established concrete, measurable tasks to evaluate Herb's progress, first in monthly and later in semiannual segments. Conservatively ramped up so as not to overwhelm or push Herb beyond his reach, the tasks proceeded through increasingly higher levels of complexity. The following examples demonstrate this progression:

Herb's Goals through March 31, 2002

- Walk short distances without support
- Walk up and down step into family room
- Use wheelchair downstairs only for sitting but not mobility
- Wear regular clothes
- Open up fingers and support right wrist.

Herb accomplished four out of the five targets within that period. The remaining one carried forward to the next six months:

Goals through September 30, 2002

- Open up fingers and support right wrist
- Get up from a seated position without help
- Walk without support from chairlift to kitchen and from upstairs chairlift to master bathroom
- Walk up and down garage ramp
- Dress self, including braces but not shoes
- When eating, pour beverage from container.

Each of these tasks requires persistent effort and practice. Sometimes the suddenness of a breakthrough thrills both of us. Steve taught his father to attach his pyramid walker to the arm of the chairlift and keep it with him as he descended to the main level. One morning Herb grew impatient waiting for me to finish a kitchen chore and decided he would do the task without my help. He pulled himself up from the lift, snapped open his walking aid, independently walked into the kitchen, and sat down in his wheelchair. A remarkable glow lit his face. *These satisfactions demonstrate that tough, exhausting, unheralded daily work is worthwhile.*

These were simple, trivial tasks before the stroke. I hadn't given them much thought because they didn't deserve any. Now I found them incredibly cumbersome, with each small step requiring significant planning and forethought. I have lost all spontaneity.

Herb continues this ritual each morning. I stand ready but do not assist except on mornings when he appears unsteady. We've had only one mishap so far. One morning he stopped at the threshold to the kitchen to scratch his nose with his left hand, forgetting this hand held the walker for balance. Although I was behind him and tried to lasso his waist, I wasn't fast enough and he crumpled onto the floor. Fortunately, he had no broken bones or massive bruises.

This short, successful trek became a baseline for subsequent tasks. Herb next tried to pull himself up from the second-floor chairlift and walk to our bedroom. Looming behind him is a flight of stairs with a fragile banister. The risk is so great that I am reluctant to let him walk alone, particularly at night, when he is tired.

This task is scary. As I get off the chair seat to initiate the walk to our master bedroom, I realize I am on the edge of a "precipice." I look down the high stairs and see open space. I know I must be extra careful here.

Mastering a single step without outside support proved difficult for both of us. Herb's weakened "good" leg sometimes twisted around his impaired right leg. I learned to lift and guide his right foot into position. Worrisome at first, it became easier with time. Today I no longer bend but gently nudge my own foot against his and push it down the step. Going up is even easier because he swings the leg into place and I use my knee to brace him. *This accomplishment is huge! It allows us to visit friends' homes and move about our own home.*

With experience comes flexibility and workable solutions. When we confront several steps without railings in other homes I plant a strong person to Herb's left side as a brace while I support his legs. Our mutual confidence continues to build. During the summer blackout of 2003, when our chairlift was inoperable, Herb held onto the banister and walked up and down our stairs with confidence.

Climbing steps, even before my stroke, had always been a task I did not cherish. My balance was poor from childhood and increasingly so with the passage of years. Now, with the stroke, I hated the chore even more and looked upon it as definitely to be avoided. But it becomes easier with practice.

My Wish List: Longer-Term Goals

Goal setting has become part of my life. You can't get to where you are going without measuring where you have been. While it is unrealistic to expect that Herb will again mow the lawn, cut the hedges, or climb a ladder to remove the storm windows, he can and will do more as the years advance. We have much further to go in our recovery journey. However, I emphasize shorter-term, more manageable markers. My goals for the coming year are basic and, if accomplished, will help me feel as though I am the luckiest woman in my limited world. Success will mean that Herb does the following:

- Performs the bed exercises without assistance
- Dresses himself in the morning even when we are rushed
- Rises from bed and walks to the toilet by himself
- Stands at the toilet (and we throw out all the urinals!)
- Discards the wheelchair or uses it rarely in the kitchen
- Performs his outside fitness routine three days a week

- Walks an average of three hundred feet daily
- Places his dishes in the sink
- Feeds the animals
- Avoids another stroke.

Enforced Independence

Herb accepts change reluctantly. The wheelchair, for example, threatened to become a permanent nesting place. His therapists cautioned that over reliance on the wheelchair for long periods leads to a permanent slouch. After many months I mapped a strategy. First, I left his footrests in the car trunk and then the full chair, claiming it was easier for me to prepare for outside appointments. Herb gradually and grumblingly adjusted to a cushioned kitchen chair for several hours at a time, which led the way to comfortable transfers to chairs in friends' homes, restaurants, and even the theater. Now that the transit chair remains permanently in the trunk, Herb is reluctant to give up his big wheelchair because it allows him to roll independently from kitchen to computer. He says he also finds it more comfortable than regular chairs.

Formerly right-handed, Herb is learning—very slowly—to compensate with his left hand. Motivated to fill in his crossword puzzles, which are intellectually very stimulating, he has developed a labored but functional pattern of cursive writing and printing.

Even from the beginning he had no problem eating. Although I still cut up difficult entrées, Herb is usually self-reliant when it comes to food, especially food he likes. He can tear the wrapping off a miniature chocolate, pour milk and iced tea, and open and close lightly capped bottles.

Independent dressing still prompts occasional tears of frustration on both our parts. The process is tedious and I prefer not to watch. Except for his heavy shoes, Herb now dresses himself. Undressing is another matter.

This undressing and dressing by myself may seem like normal chores—but they're not. Each time I try to put on my socks and sleeveless undershirt

the pain in my right cheek intensifies. This rocks me and persists for hours. As a limiting factor it turns small chores into detestable tasks.

Even though independent dressing sometimes brings on facial pain, it offers Herb another notch toward independence and lightens my load. Finding a balance between compassion and resolve is tough. I think we need another crash session with an occupational therapist to move this process along.

The need to do things on my own is overrated. Sometimes I don't care about self-improvement and just want these tasks done for me. The urge to continually improve is not a burden I wish to carry.

Perhaps the biggest breakthrough of all is Herb's increasing ability to handle the urinal and free me from a less favored responsibility. Now I can disappear for an hour or two, either into a different room or away from the house. We haven't reached the point where Herb will roll himself to the refrigerator and prepare his own lunch. But he didn't do that before his stroke. Perhaps one day, if he is hungry enough, he may yet put together a meal. But of all the possible tasks, this one remains the least probable.

Stumbling Blocks

Depression sometimes hangs heavy, and tears of frustration and waves of self-pity spring up without warning. When this happens, we pull the plugs and cancel most of our plans. Herb retreats to his green recliner or bed and sleeps away the afternoon. But there are now more good days than bad. *I am impatient with these setbacks. "Active listening," gently reiterating his statements to better understand his mood, wins points with psychologists but is something I don't do well. I know I need to listen better and respond with "What makes you say that?" but his depression turns me off, especially when the pattern accelerates over several days or weeks.*

Hers is a terrible dilemma. I cannot help feeling that between these two extremes of apathy and hope, she is caught in my net. A stroke is the pits. I can think of no good things that result from it. But there are four factors that

have kept me from losing my mind: the array of therapies, inside and outside our home and their regularity; the computer for communicating; outside activities and quality of life pursuits, like the Shaw Festival; and my wife.

Reluctantly Returning Autonomy

Herb had a particularly bad setback toward the middle of the third poststroke year. Observing our continuing clash of wills over exercise, his psychologist suggested Herb assume responsibility for his full rehab program and outside pursuits. *This huge step toward independence worried me because I suspected he would choose the easy way and reject further fitness activities.* Exhausted myself, I reluctantly agreed to the plan. Initial results confirmed my forebodings. Within two weeks of lapsed exercise, Herb fell while standing in place as I opened the outside door to the patio. *I bit my tongue and chose not to comment. It was tough to watch and not jump up and down, saying, "I told you so!"*

Herb pushed himself less and retreated into a steady regimen of television and puzzles. This free fall continued for six months while I, feeling like a hapless bystander, watched his strength and endurance diminish. He had less energy, slept more, and retreated further into a shell. The fitness program dwindled from three times a week to one. This bad stretch prompted me to arrange a joint tour through the nearby assisted living facility mentioned earlier. I felt Herb needed to know where I draw my line and that I choose to continue as his caregiver only as long as he pushes himself to improve.

We entered the fourth year with two new incentives: Steve's visit and our treadmill. Steve and I stood in front of the treadmill and talked so much about minimizing risk that Herb became impatient and demanded we begin. To my surprise and amazement, he took to it right away and has been pushing himself steadily ever since. He likes the idea that he controls his own limits and strives for increasingly longer periods with each session. Within the first six weeks he progressed from one to fourteen minutes and would have pushed even further had both Otis and I not protested.

The treadmill introduces another challenge to the bewildering array of exercises that I must do every day. There are two variables to be confronted. The first

simply has to do with the amount of time I'm on the machine; when I began it was only about three minutes. The second is the speed at which the treadmill was set. Originally, it was calibrated at the lowest possible speed, at about 0.3 miles per hour. Now I have it at 0.8.

The treadmill opens the way to Herb's less grudging acceptance of other exercises that build strength and endurance. With few exceptions, Herb now follows a consistent weekly exercise schedule: three days on the treadmill and two at the fitness center. Each activity, which takes under one hour, still wears him out. Exercise will never be my husband's favorite pursuit, but it has a prominent place in our life today, and even he admits he sees progress.

Herb's energy and determination spill over to other areas. He is much less apt to use passive grunting and pointing, and he is more forthcoming in asking directly for what he wants. His increasing self-reliance frees me from feeling like an unappreciated servant, and I more eagerly apply my energy to areas and projects I find revitalizing. *Our relationship is not perfect, but it's improving.*

I cope better now with Herb's changeable moods because the dark ones do not hang on as long as they did previously. When one or both of us becomes mercurial, a break seems to work.

A Progress Report

Health-wise, Herb appears stabilized. Medication, exercise, and diet combine to maintain his blood sugar well within normal limits, albeit with the boost of oral medication. His color is good, and he looks much like himself prior to the stroke. He receives continuing good reports from his neurologist, cardiologist, and internist. Although vigilance and prevention efforts never cease, follow-up medical visits are now relegated to quarterly and semiannual appointments.

Sleep apnea is no longer an issue *(at least for Herb—I wear ear plugs).* Facial pain has lessened but not disappeared. Even the urinary disturbance is less troubling. Without a doubt Depend, my lifesaver, facilitates our public outings.

Herb's speech has improved significantly. Those not accustomed to his vocal patterns understand at least 90 percent of what he says either in direct conversation or over the telephone. He willingly engages in conversation across the dinner table and voices opinions about current events. During a museum tour in Pittsburgh with friends, toward the end of year three, he asked several questions of the tour leader, his first in a public forum since the stroke. While he still has not raised a question in our seminars, I remain hopeful his powerful curiosity will overcome reluctant self-consciousness.

Speaking will be a continuous problem because it requires special deference from my fellow listeners. Most importantly, they must realize my deficiencies and allow me to speak my peace without interruption.

The local business journal has printed several of Herb's opinion columns since the stroke, and he is searching for other outlets. We attend concerts, plays, and other easily accessible cultural programs. *I still prefer the easy way and choose matinees, recognizing how much time it takes at the end of the evening to undress and prepare Herb for bed. But even this concern is abating, and we've not shied away from selected evening events.*

An overall routine has set in as we get on with our lives. Even hard tasks are easier now that they are better established.

I have begun to resume my own identity. *That by itself presents another challenge, but one I alone must address.* In the meantime, I apply my energy to writing, gardening, home improvement projects, and anything else that comes my way. For the second time in three years, I blacktopped our long driveway while Otis remained with Herb. This time I addressed the task not from anger but resourcefulness: the asphalt was cracking and I chose to save money. Quiet time on a cool spring morning allowed me to think about future needs, reshape parts of this manuscript, and clear my mind. I liked the challenge.

Otis has become a member of our family, and I rely upon him increasingly for my support as well as Herb's. His patience and good humor allow me to take respite breaks twice a year. On occasions when Herb is depressed and uncooperative with me, he usually is in good form with Otis and can joke with him.

We're an unlikely pair. Otis, who is African American, is a jack-of-all-trades and serves as my caretaker-friend. We have become very close.

Our situation, although it has improved dramatically, is not without friction. The stroke forced Herb to admit he will never drive again. He navigates and I drive. During heavy rainstorms and spurts of intense traffic, he's become a cranky side-seat driver who punctuates his thoughts and grimaces with pregnant silence, *especially when I need directions.* It's obvious he feels he can perform better than I. *Had I the choice to turn over the steering wheel in inclement weather and late at night, I would. But if I don't drive, we simply won't get where we want to go. Both of us must accept this as a fact of life and move on.*

These trips are traumatic. I had been driving for over forty years, and now I must sit on the passenger side. My abbreviated skills require me to make interesting chatter, give directions (which is a useless function with my wife), and point out the sights. I was not a macho driver, but I still felt that the driving chore was essentially mine.

Lessons Learned

Set goals.

Recorded goal setting is valuable because it leaves a measurable trail. You know where you are going because you build on where you've been.

You can't save someone who doesn't want to be saved.

You can fight for your loved one, slay dragons, battle the medical and insurance establishments, and handle all the daily necessities. But unless your stroke patient can conquer depression and is willing to move forward, you'll find yourself spinning in circles. The effort has to be shared. If not, the caregiver must learn to walk away, emotionally as well as physically. That is truly tough love.

Fight for life and wellness.

It doesn't come automatically. Most survivors will probably seek the easiest way and simply live on a day-to-day basis. They need a push.

Search for pilot therapy programs.

If you live near a medical school or teaching hospital or are a veteran, check with their stroke departments to see whether they offer studies in which your survivor might participate. Also search the Internet.

Seek cultural programs with matinee performances.

As you make your way back into the world, find programs that are compatible with your schedule and achievable without great stress. Matinees offer afternoon performances and daytime driving.

Return autonomy to your stroke survivor.

Hovering and helping too much aren't good for either the stroke survivor or the caregiver. The return of power, decision making, and responsibility is very tough but necessary for both. You must learn to let go.

Don't feel you have to use all the advice that professionals offer.

Value your own judgment and common sense. Adapt those suggestions that work for you in your situation. Discard the others.

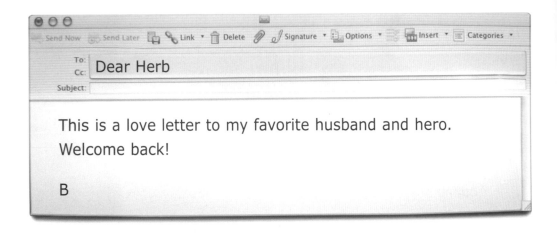

To: **Dear Herb**
Cc:
Subject:

This is a love letter to my favorite husband and hero.
Welcome back!

B

CHAPTER 19
Conclusion

There Is No Vision as Perfect as Hindsight

Nothing in our previous lives prepared us for the challenges of cataclysmic illness. Caught in the grip of stroke, Herb and I forced ourselves to search for strength and hope in each other and in a higher power with greater capacity than ours. From the beginning, I believed that Herb could and would improve. While the stroke might ravage his body, I pledged I would not allow it to destroy his mind and spirit. My toughest job all along has been to convince him to push forward despite all the obvious obstacles.

Herb's Report Card

We are now just beyond our three-year juncture, and it is time for an honest assessment. Was the post-recovery effort worth our huge commitment? My answer swings back and forth each day and sometimes week, depending upon the degree of Herb's facial pain and his mood.[66] Lately, however, while he has periodic regressions the hopelessness no longer dominates.

---

[66] *I have rewritten this conclusion many times as both our moods repeatedly rose and sank.*

I grow more optimistic as I watch Herb's progress and willingness to engage in conversation with me. I see my husband slowly but steadily reemerging, and that gives me confidence that sometime in the future I may yet regain my companion and best friend. This awareness sweeps away all the hard work and doubts that preceded it. Yes, I would do it again! But I hope not to, and that is the reason I work so hard.

I'm not sure. Sometimes, when I'm outside, the world looks the same, kind of. When I'm inside, everything is constrained by my very limited world. My daily routine subdivides into physical therapy exercises, toileting, eating (I've lost the freedom to choose which foods I really like and which I thoroughly detest), and even spending time at the computer is boring. I must find something challenging to occupy me.

There will always be shadows because a survivor requires great vigilance to guard against another stroke. But with steady hard work we've learned that incremental improvements lead to larger ones. We are fortunate to build on a foundation of forty-plus years of shared obstinacy and willpower along with mutual trust, respect, and love. These fundamentals are forged even stronger today. The strength of our relationship fuels the engine for even greater recovery.

We have learned many hard and humbling lessons in our journey back to the world of the living. We share these openly so that our experiences, for better or worse, may ease the way for tens of thousands of upcoming caregivers and survivors who will travel through the same stroke underworld each year. The most profound of all lessons learned is our realization that at no time, even at points of our greatest despair, did we struggle alone or in isolation.

I still am ambivalent. Especially on those long, wintry days and nights I wonder what I'm doing here. Sometimes it seems like we are on a continuum to nowhere; sometimes I have more hope.

It Takes a Cosmos

More than our own efforts, we have benefited from the support, kindness, and wisdom of so many others who surround us. Senator Hillary Clinton believes it takes a village to raise a child. I claim it takes a cosmos to save one stroke victim, namely, my husband.

If not for the U.S. taxpayers (Medicare) and AARP supplemental insurance, we would have been financially devastated and unable to pay the huge medical and therapy expenses to save Herb's life and restore some of his function.

If not for the teams of physicians who battled to save Herb's life and continue to address strange problems we encounter along the way, he would have become locked into a useless body.

If not for the researchers who persevere in new breakthroughs for treating stroke survivors, we would have no hope or basis for continuing improvement.

If not for our rehabilitation psychologist, Herb would be dispirited and isolated. He and I would no doubt be divorced at this point, both thoroughly depressed and defeated by the huge adjustment to a vastly curtailed life.

If not for our teams of speech, physical, and occupational therapists, Herb would be as the stroke left him, unable to move, communicate, or care for many of his personal needs.

If not for our respite care and home team with their gentle, cajoling resourcefulness, we would be at each other's throats constantly. Or perhaps even in adjacent rooms in a nearby nursing home.

If not for friends and neighbors, we would be isolated and overwhelmed in every aspect of this huge battle.

If not for prayers said around the world, we would be alone and greatly weakened.

If not for our children and close family members, we would lack support and sustaining love.

If not for Steve, I would not have known where to even begin our poststroke efforts.

If not for each other, we would not have tried.

If not for God, we would have no hope.

So, yes, there is room for hope. We believe Herb will improve and be one of the 58 percent of male stroke survivors who do not have a second stroke within five years of the first. In the meantime, each day adds greater promise.

Lessons Learned

Survival builds on hope, stamina on progress.

You can't give up.

Recovery requires a cosmos.

A vast community of resources, love, and support buoy our own small efforts.

POSTSCRIPT

April 2005

Herb and I are rapidly approaching the four-year poststroke marker and our forty-second anniversary. Both achievements are only two weeks apart. We tally obvious accomplishments as we move along: Herb is now at 1.0 mph on his treadmill and advancing slowly but steadily. A recent brain scan indicates significant improvement in blood velocity (the results are termed "astounding" by his current neurologist), which I attribute to both GRECC programs.

Herb has also had another op-ed column published in the local business journal, "Climate Not Conducive to High-Tech Hopes." He also added many more comments to this manuscript when he realized it would be published. All along his most jaundiced comment was, "Who is the audience to read this?" Now he knows.

On the negative side, his facial pain has ratcheted up again to sometimes curtail active exercise. Although we may take a day or two off, we return to schedule. Very cold feet and legs present another worrisome problem. We've taken to elevating both his feet in the evening as Herb sits at the table, reading and watching TV. We've called it to our internist's attention, and Herb will undergo various tests in future months.

And yes, we've had the fall. Last November Herb exited the car with my help and, following our regular routine, stood with his walker while he waited for me to pull the car farther into our garage and park. Avidly listening to the OSU–Michigan football game on the car radio, he involuntarily shifted his positioning and fell face forward on the concrete garage floor. *Never in the history of the world has there been so much blood.*

I ran into the house, raced out with Steve's bench, and working together we pulled him back to a standing position so that he could walk up the ramp. Once he was seated in the house with an icepack, I contacted the triage nurse, who urged me to bring him to the emergency room immediately for a CAT scan. Apparently, a forceful blow to the head by a person taking both aspirin and plavix can cause brain hemorrhage.

Fortunately, the results were negative. Herb looked like a raccoon for a couple of weeks but recovered fully. It required several months for my own nervous system to get back in sync. I now more cautiously leave the car in idle while I walk him up the ramp. We've managed to avoid more of the awful falls that plague stroke survivors, but this reminder is sobering enough to make us both more cautious.

Herb and I continue to battle the "get me to a nursing home" syndrome, which emerges once in a while. My latest response is, *"Sure. When do you want to go?"* In general, I prefer to brush off these regressions because, in aggregate, we are moving forward. Once again we hold tickets for the Shaw and Stratford festivals, and plan to meet family at one and Milwaukee friends at the other.

I've had more episodes of my own recurrent pain and retain a loose-leaf book filled with varied prognostications from the specialists.[67] These attacks generally occur when I feel tired and run-down. I am also working hard to gain more of an independent existence. I have become involved in publishing our book, taken on additional writing projects, and given over increasing responsibility to Otis. My sojourn at the spa in Ixtapan, Mexico, with my New York friends has become an annual event, and I eagerly look forward to each January.

Herb has reclaimed many quality-of-life pursuits and is now, thanks to our encouraging psychologist, composing remembrances on the word processor that may well become his own book. Although he fears boredom, he is still reluctant to become more proactive. My role as a facilitator, advocate, and wife continues. But after four years I prefer to turn responsibility as initiator back to my husband. Herb is a bright man and able to assume increased responsibility for independent pursuits. Perhaps one day he may find himself inspired, or bored, enough to Google "wheelchair vacations" and plan a trip for us. That challenge is one to grow on.

---

[67] *In desperation, because episodes averaged one per month, I resolved (with my internist's blessing) to stop all prescription drugs (except for my asthma medications) and over-the-counter vitamins. These attacks quieted almost immediately.*

Now where do we go? I don't think my situation will change much over the next few years. The biggest fear I have is boredom—ennui, which can suck me dry of new ideas and drain old favorites. Although I'm limited physically, I still want to continue the pursuit of intellectual pleasure we had once planned for. We'll see.

It's not Kansas, as Dorothy in the *Wizard of Oz* might say, but it's not bad either. We've come a long way.

ACKNOWLEDGMENTS
Key Participants in Our Journey

We have many people to thank for their strength and support on our difficult journey. We begin with our family: our daughters and son, Kathryn, Miriam, and Steve Kleiman; our niece, Anne Kleiman; William and Thérèse Kleiman, Herb's brother and our sister-in-law; Alan and Lois Elkin, Berenice's brother and our sister-in-law.

Our home crew provided inspiration and support: Sara Kass, "surrogate" daughter, trainer, friend; Otis Bush, respite caregiver and friend; Anna Debrogorski, home physical therapist; John Lee and Nora Sherwin, tai chi instructors; Deborah Lief, trainer; Henry Miles, handyman and craftsman in charge of all things that need fixing; and Conor Willis, dog walker extraordinaire. We deeply appreciate the sage financial guidance provided by our accountant, Joyce Graham, and our broker, Don Jacobson.

We are grateful to our family, friends, and professionals who read rough drafts of this manuscript and shared comments and critique: Laurie and Aaron Billowitz; Elizabeth Dreben; Sim and Dov Goobich; Kathy Grekco; Mary Jo Hoff; Miriam Kleiman; Ethel Morrison; Bill Pitt, founder of the Cleveland Stroke Club; Tena Rosner; Maxine Schinagle; Eran Shiloh; Naomi Soifer; Susan Golden; and Alan Weiss. Michael Felver wrote the foreword and provided editorial support and medical terminology. Marc Golub generously donated his time and expertise to establish our web site, www.onestroketwosurvivors.com—and also provided photography, digital scanning and retouching. Fred Reiner, a dear friend from Baltimore, provided the cover image. Beth Brumbaugh and Greg Hackett thoughtfully contributed the treadmill that keeps Herb moving forward.

We extend special thanks to the professionals we hold in good standing for reaching beyond the minimum and pulling us through some very difficult problems: Stanley Beekman, DPM, podiatric physician and surgeon; Miriam Cohen, MD, Heart Associates Inc. at Union Memorial Hospital, Baltimore; Elizabeth Dreben, PhD, Rehabilitation Psychologist,

MetroHealth Medical Center; Michael Felver, MD, Dept. of Internal Medicine, Cleveland Clinic Foundation; Michael Frankel, MD, Gastroenterology Associates of Cleveland; Brian Garrity, PT, the Claude D. Pepper Center, GRECC, University of Maryland; Andrew P. Goldberg, MD, Professor of Medicine at the University of Maryland School of Medicine and Director of the Claude D. Pepper Older Americans Independence Center; Karen Kahn, DDS, Dept. of Dentistry, Cleveland Clinic Foundation; Anne Kleiman, DO, Associate Attending in Neurology, Metropolitan Hospital, NYC; Richard Macko, MD, Associate Professor of Neurology at the University of Maryland School of Medicine and director of the stroke progress program at the Baltimore VA; Asikin Mentari, MD, Dept. of Rehabilitation, MetroHealth Medical Center; Kathleen Michael, PhD, RN, CRRN, Program Manager, the Claude D. Pepper Center, GRECC, University of Maryland; Peter Rasmussen, MD, Dept. of Neurosurgery, Cleveland Clinic Foundation; David Sholitan, MD, Dept. of Ophthalmology, Cleveland Clinic Foundation; Jill Whitall, PhD, Associate Professor of Physical Therapy at the University of Maryland School of Medicine and stroke progress program leader; Nishan Tambay, MD, formerly of the Dept. of Rehabilitation, MetroHealth Medical Center; Alan Weiss, MD, Dept. of Internal Medicine, Cleveland Clinic Foundation.

And I reserve special thoughts for my toughest critic, my guide, manuscript editor, and graphic designer, Steve Kleiman.

APPENDIX A
Words to Know

Charcot-Marie-Tooth disease
A progressive neuromuscular disorder that mainly affects the limbs.

cholesterol
A form of blood fat that may settle into artery walls.

diabetes
A chronic disease marked by high levels of sugar in the blood.

Hb A1c
A test that measures the amount of glycosylated hemoglobin in the blood. The test gives a good estimate of how well diabetes is being managed over time.

HDL — High-density lipoprotein
The "good" cholesterol, best if above 50.

hematocrit
The percentage of whole blood comprised of red blood cells.

hematoma
An accumulation of blood in tissue, usually caused by trauma.

hemiparesis
Weakness or partial paralysis on one side of the body.

LDL — Low-density lipoprotein
The "bad" cholesterol, except if below 100.

lipid (a)
A lipoprotein associated with vascular damage; may be genetically linked.

lipid profile

A measure of the level of various fats in the blood.

Medicare Part A

Medicare coverage for inpatient costs in hospitals and skilled nursing facilities.

Medicare Part B

Medicare coverage of physician services, outpatient hospital care, and some other medical services that Part A does not cover.

MRA — Magnetic resonance angiogram

An MRI procedure that assesses the patterning of intracranial vessels and whether arteries inside the skull are clogged.

MRI — Magnetic resonance imaging

A noninvasive procedure that uses powerful magnets and radio waves and is particularly useful for the brain. The patient is asked to lie on a narrow table that slides into a large tunnel-like tube within the scanner.

OT

Occupational therapists help people improve their basic motor functions and perform tasks in daily living and work environments.

PT

Physical therapists help restore function, improve mobility, relieve pain, and prevent or limit permanent physical disabilities of patients suffering from injuries or disease.

ST

Speech therapists help people with speech problems to shape thoughts into words and communicate ideas.

stroke

An interruption of the blood supply to any part of the brain, resulting in damaged brain tissue. Stroke is the third leading cause of death in most developed countries, and the leading cause of disability in adults. Most strokes are due to blood clots that block blood flow.

TIA — Transient ischemic attack

Caused by an interruption of blood flow to brain cells causing strokelike symptoms that resolve within twenty-four hours; if the symptoms do not resolve completely, the event is called a stroke.

tPA — Tissue plasminogen activator

Injected intravenously, it activates enzymes that can dissolve a blood clot in an hour or two; if tPA is given within the first two to three hours of stroke onset, it may reduce permanent disability; in rare cases, the treatment may result in internal bleeding.

APPENDIX B
Useful Resources on the Internet

There is excellent information about stroke-related issues from worldwide resources on the Internet. The following well-documented websites are useful, but we urge caution in your searches because abundant misinformation circulates on the Web. Corroborate information with established medical and governmental sites. Because caregivers have little time or inclination for research,[68] you may want to ask others to conduct the search for you. Here are a few sites we think are worthwhile.

One Stroke, Two Survivors website
http://www.onestroketwosurvivors.com
A working guide for stroke survival

The Cleveland Clinic
http://www.clevelandclinic.org/health
A broad range of health support

National Stroke Association
http://www.stroke.org
Lists studies, new information, and support

American Stroke Association
http://www.strokeassociation.org
Includes programs, caregivers' support

The Stroke Network
http://www.strokenetwork.org
An on-line support group with message board and chat room

National Institutes of Health/National Institute of Neurological Disorders and Stroke (NINDS)
http://www.ninds.nih.gov/disorders/stroke/stroke.htm
Basic details about stroke

---

[68] *Other than researching basic stroke complications I had little time for the Internet in our first two poststroke years.*

Internet Stroke Center at Washington University in St. Louis

http://www.strokecenter.org/education/rx_complications/2.html
Preventing and managing stroke complications

Chronic Pain after Stroke

http://www.painrelieffoundation.org.uk/paininfo/pain_cpsp.html
Good background reading

Diabetes and Stroke

http://my.webmd.com/context/article/46/1667_50942.htm
Good background reading

Complications of Stroke

http://www.wrongdiagnosis.com/s/stroke/complic.htm
Good background reading

Pharmaceutical Support

http://www.rxassist.org
http://www.needymeds.com
Special pharmaceutical programs

Canadian Drugstore

http://www.canadiandrugstore.com
Ordering online from RxNorth

Caregiver's Bill of Rights

http://www.mindspring.com/~tscotent/bill.htm
Guidelines for protection of caregivers

APPENDIX C
Herbert S. Kleiman Daily Medications

Here is one of our prepared information sheets we bring to medical and dental appointments. Information compiled on one sheet is an efficient way to avoid the first fifteen minutes of an appointment usually given to discussing and recording medications. I find this tool valuable and rely on its accuracy when I fill Herb's medicine boxes every two weeks because it lists medications, dosages, time of day and name of prescribing physician (for new medications).

8:00 a.m.

PILLS

Plavix	1	75 mg per Dr. D. Hammer 1/03
Metoprolol (Lopressor)	1/2	25 mg
Glyburide	1	5 mg
Glucophage (metformin)	1	850 mg
Lisinopril (Zestril)	1/2	5 mg
Nitroglycerin capsule	1	6.5 mg per Dr. M. Cohen, 5/2/02
MiraLax	daily	1 measured capful
Celexa	1	40 mg per Dr. Weiss 6/2/03
Centrum Silver vitamin	1	Per Dr. Weiss

INHALATION

Advair Diskus	1 spray	100/50

(continued)

4:00–6:00 p.m.

PILLS

Nitroglycerin capsule	1	6.5 mg per Dr. M. Cohen, 5/2/02
Glyburide	1/2	2.5 mg
Tricor (every other day)	1	54 mg Per Dr. Sprecher, 4/15/02 per Dr. Cohen, 1/04
Foltx sf/df	1	25 mg folic acid
Cozaar	1	25 mg per Dr. Cohen, 1/04
Aspirin	1	81 mg/coated aspirin

9:00–10:00 p.m.

PILLS

Metoprolol (Lopressor)	1/2	25 mg
Trazodone	1	100 mg as needed for sleep

INHALATION

Advair Diskus	1 spray	100/50

APPENDIX D
Herbert S. Kleiman Summary Sheet

Here is one of our prepared information sheets from Herb's loose-leaf medical file that I carry on trips and distribute at all new medical and therapy appointments. A medical history at one glance avoids lots of repetitive questions. I also keep a separate file for my own records.

Patient's Comprehensive Medical History

- Charcot-Marie-Tooth disease (since childhood but diagnosed in 1973)
- Type 2 diabetes mellitus, diagnosed in 1983
- Asthma, diagnosed in 1977
- Hypercholesterolemia
- Stroke-related severe right hemiparesis re 7/14/01
- Stents (2) arteriosclerosis re 3/18/02
- Transfusions (2) re iron deficiency anemia on 5/10/02
- Speech prosthesis with pharyngeal wax; consult and initial steps begin 2/26; monthly buildup through Sept. 13, 2002; prosthesis discontinued at that time. NO PRIOR FACIAL PAIN.
- FACIAL PAIN begins approximately mid-September 2002; panoramic film by Cleve. Clinic dentistry dept. on 9/25/02 indicates no dental pathology.
- Subsequent visits and assessments with 3 Cleveland Clinic neurologists, including a specialist in trigeminal neuralgia; 3 dentists including general, periodontist, endodontist (2 unrelated root canals); Cleveland Clinic Pain Center including a nerve block; 4 sets of acupuncture through MetroHealth Medical Center. Neurontin and Trileptal found to offer no benefit. No diagnosis other than atypical facial pain.
- Pain continues and ranges on scale from 1–8 with increasing intensity over last 4 months.

(continued)

Recent Stroke History

7/14/01   Patient has first stroke. Admitted to Cleveland Clinic.

7/17/01   Worsening of right hemiparesis and dysarthria: emergency angiography.

7/17/01   Stents inserted into carotid and left middle cerebral arteries.

7/26/01   Patient transferred to MetroHealth Stroke Rehabilitation acute care.

8/28/01   Discharged from MetroHealth Hospital to home.

9/4/01–10/1/01   Home nursing care including nursing, physical, occupational, and speech (minimal) therapies.

9/11/01   Cleveland Clinic emergency room visit due to muscular spasms in arms and pain in left shoulder. Demonstrated emotional distress related to national calamity on this day. Examination reveals no heart problem, but a urinary tract infection. Patient is discharged without overnight stay. With prescription for Bactrim.

9/14/01   Cleveland Clinic emergency room visit due to dehydration and exhaustion. Patient is admitted for one night observation and extensive blood/ultrasound testing. Prescription changed to Cipro.

9/18/01   Patient passes modified barium swallow study (4th effort) and is advised to receive ENT evaluation for suspected vocal cord paralysis.

10/02/01   Patient begins outpatient therapy at MetroHealth Stroke Rehabilitation Center.

3/18/02   Cardiac angioplasty with 2 stents at Cleveland Clinic.

APPENDIX E
Medications as of 3/16/04

This concise list of Herb's medications and dosages offers both a safety mechanism[69] and a brief summary at a certain point in recovery.

Herbert Kleiman Medications as of 3/16/04

Plavix	75 mg
Metoprolol	25 mg (1/2 tablet 2x)
Glyburide	5 mg tablet (1 1/2x per day)
Glucophage	850 mg tablet
Nitroglycerin	6.5 capsule (2x per day)
Celexa	40 mg tablet
Cozaar	25 mg tablet
Lisinopril	10 mg tablet (1/2 per day)
Aspirin	81 mg tablet
Trazodone	100 mg tablet
Advair Diskus	100/50 (2 sprays 2x)
Tricor	54 mg (every other day)
Foltx	25 mg folic acid
MiraLax	1 capful daily
Centrum Silver	1 daily

---

[69] *The physician can see at a glance all the medications. This method helps to avoid problems with new prescriptions that might be contraindicated and also helps to discard any that are no longer required.*

APPENDIX F
Memo of 5/18/02 to Physician Team

Frustrated that the many specialists did not communicate with one another and/or appeared unaware of Herb's multiple complications, I devised this summary memo. My bottom line was that I required each physician on this list to send all subsequent reports, tests, and memos to our internist and me.

> **RE:** Patient—Herbert S. Kleiman (Clinic #; MHC #; Soc. Sec. #)
> **TO:** Drs. (listed by name, phone number, and fax)
> **SUBJECT:** Coordination and Communication
>
> We are fortunate to have a health care team of wonderful, very caring professionals and friends who are working to establish a higher quality of life for Herb Kleiman, following his stroke on July 14, 2001, and stenting in mid-March 2002. You represent four different hospital systems within two states. In an attempt to update Herb's records, improve communication, and avoid duplication of effort, please note the following:
>
> - Dr. Alan Weiss, listed above, has replaced Dr. Michael Felver as Herb's internist and team coordinator, effective immediately. **All procedures, blood tests, and results should go through Dr. Weiss with copies to me.** Dr. Felver, who has an aggressive travel schedule, has kindly agreed to remain as an adviser.
> - Dr. Miriam Cohen, cardiologist, Union Memorial Hospital in Baltimore, provided a second opinion in late April. She performed a persantine nuclear stress test. A summary including corresponding blood work is available through Dr. Weiss (or me). The result: although there is diffuse ASCVD with severe 3-vessel coronary artery disease—with stents in the RCA and LAD, the situation is now stabilized. Because of Herb's many medical problems and the fact that he is virtually asymptomatic from a cardiac standpoint at this time, medical management rather than bypass surgery should be optimized and continued.
> - Of concern, however, were both a hematocrit of 28 with 6 percent iron saturation, which indicates slow blood loss, and a white count of 13,000.

Dr. Cohen recommended that Herb be seen immediately by both his urologist and gastroenterologist. She further prescribed a long-acting nitro capsule, 6.5 mg, 2 x per day and recommended that he have another persantine nuclear stress test in 4–6 months, depending on his clinical status.

- Dr. Michael Frankel, gastroenterologist, reviewed Dr. Cohen's analysis. Prior to initiating both endoscopic and colonoscopic procedures, he arranged for the transfusion of 2 units of blood on May 10, 2002, at Hillcrest Hospital, and began a series of 16 iron injections (2 per week for 8 weeks).

- Dr. Martin Resnick cultured Herb's urine and on May 16 reported evidence of gram positive bacteria, with >100,000 colonies of Group D Strep, nonenterococcus. He prescribed ampicillin, 250 mg, for 10 days followed by a second culture.

- Dr. Weiss assumed management of Herb's case on May 13. He has reviewed all past records, including Dr. Cohen's results, and added chronic sinusitis to the lengthy list of ailments. He prescribed Flonase 0.05 percent nasal spray (one puff per 1x per day)—and recommended eliminating Actos, Ditropan, and Remeron from Herb's list of meds.

- Dr. John Perl II, endovascular neurosurgery, ordered a follow-up CAT scan to monitor any repeating stenosis of the brain. This was conducted yesterday, 5/17 at the clinic along with a CBC. He will issue a report on Monday, May 20. Dr. Perl will be moving out of state the end of May and will refer Herb to a successor.

That sums up activity for the past two weeks. Please, folks, it is absolutely necessary that specialist members of this team coordinate with Dr. Weiss, confer with one another, and share results and perhaps conflicts, before overlapping. Telephone and fax numbers are provided above. I further require copies of all written records faxed to me at (phone #) as a fail-safe.

Again Herb and I thank all of you from the bottom of our hearts for reaching out and performing such Herculean efforts to not only keep him alive but in hope of achieving continuing progress.

Sincerely,

Berenice Kleiman

APPENDIX G
Suggested Readings

There are few available and inspiring books about stroke survivors from a firsthand perspective. Bauby's *The Diving Bell and the Butterfly* is particularly poignant and inspirational because it is written by a paralyzed stroke victim who could move only one eye. He died one day before his book was published. Also included on my list is a range of books that provide background and support.

Bauby, Jean-Dominique. *The Diving Bell and the Butterfly: A Memoir of Life in Death*. New York: Knopf, 1997.

Carter, Rosalynn, with Susan K. Golant. *Helping Someone with Mental Illness: A Compassionate Guide for Family, Friends, and Caregivers.* New York: Crown, 1998.

Doka, Kenneth J. *Living with Life-Threatening Illness: A Guide for Patients, Their Families, and Caregivers.* New York: Lexington Books, 1993.

Edsall, Susan. *Into the Blue: A Father's Flight and a Daughter's Return.* New York: St. Martin's Press, 2004.

Josephs, Arthur. *The Invaluable Guide to Life after Stroke: An Owner's Manual.* Long Beach, CA: Amadeus Press, 1992.

McCrum, Robert. *My Year Off: Recovering Life after a Stroke.* New York: W. W. Norton, 1998.

Napier, Kristine. *Eat Away Diabetes: Beat Type 2 Diabetes by Winning the Blood Sugar Battle.* New York: Prentice Hall Press, 2002.

Ornish, Dean. *Dr. Dean Ornish's Program for Reversing Heart Disease: The Only System Scientifically Proven to Reverse Heart Disease Without Drugs or Surgery.* New York: Ballantine Books, 1995.

———. *Everyday Cooking with Dr. Dean Ornish: 150 Easy, Low-Fat, High-Flavor Recipes.* New York: HarperCollins, 2002.

Paullin, Ellen. *Ted's Stroke: The Caregiver's Story.* Cabin John, MD: Seven Locks Press, 1988.

Senelick, Richard C., Peter W. Rossi, and Karla Dougherty. *Living with Stroke: A Guide for Families.* 3rd ed. Chicago: Contemporary Books, 2001.

Simopoulos, Artemis P., and Jo Robinson. *The Omega Diet: The Lifesaving Nutritional Program Based on the Diet of the Island of Crete.* New York: HarperCollins, 1999.